INDIAN INFANTICIDE

INDIAN INFANTICIDE

ITS ORIGIN, PROGRESS, AND SUPPRESSION

JOHN CAVE BROWNE, M. A.

GYAN

Published by

Gyan Publishing House
5, Ansari Road
Daryaganj, New Delhi-110002
Phone: 011-47034999, 9811692060
E-mail: books@gyanbooks.com

Distribution Network
gyanbooks.com
India, USA, Canada, UK, Australia, France

ISBN: 978-81-212-8678-7 (PB)
First Published, 1857

2nd Impression 2023

Printed at: Gyan Press, Delhi.

INDIAN INFANTICIDE
Author: John Cave Browne

INDIAN INFANTICIDE:

ITS ORIGIN, PROGRESS, AND SUPPRESSION.

BY JOHN CAVE BROWNE, M.A.,

ASSISTANT-CHAPLAIN, BENGAL ESTABLISHMENT.

. . . . . . Auditæ voces, vagitus et ingens
Infantum . . . . . .
Quas, dulcis vitæ exsortes et ab utere raptas,
Abstulit atra dies.

VIRGIL, Æn., lib. vi. l. 426—429.

LONDON:

W. H. ALLEN AND CO., LEADENHALL STREET.

1857.

TO

WILLIAM BUTTERWORTH BAYLEY, ESQ.,

TO WHOSE KINDNESS

THE AUTHOR

IS INDEBTED FOR HIS POSITION AS A

CHAPLAIN IN INDIA,

THIS WORK, ILLUSTRATING THE CHARACTER AND PROGRESS OF MEASURES

TENDING IN NO ORDINARY DEGREE

TO THE MORAL AND SOCIAL IMPROVEMENT OF THE

PEOPLE OF THAT COUNTRY,

IS DEDICATED

WITH FEELINGS OF THE DEEPEST GRATITUDE AND RESPECT.

PREFACE.

Custom seems to have given almost a prescriptive right to the public to expect something in the form of an introduction, when a new work is presented to them, while it has placed an author under a corresponding obligation to offer some prefatory remarks, either apologetic, or explanatory, or both. In the present case, this custom is the more readily complied with, that the author is altogether unknown to the public, and scarcely less so the subject of which he has attempted to treat, to a large majority of them. It is, therefore, the more necessary that he should at the outset explain why he has been induced to obtrude himself and his subject on their notice.

In the end of October, 1853, having occasion to pass through the city of Umritsur, at the time when the note of preparation was being sounded on every side for the approaching meeting for the suppression of infanticide in the

Punjab, but being unable to delay on his road in order to witness the proceedings, he could only console himself for the loss of such a gratification by endeavouring to gain some insight into the bearings of the great social question to be there discussed, which seemed to be attracting such general attention. That charming book, "Raikes's Notes on the North-Western Provinces," lent to him by a friend, most acceptably supplied the want he felt, proving a cheerful companion on his lonely journey, and explaining, as it does, in a lucid and touching manner, among other subjects of Indian interest, the system of female infanticide as practised by the Rajpoots; and, from that time, what had previously been rather a matter of curiosity became one of deep interest, which was greatly strengthened by his being enabled a few months afterwards to witness the scarcely less important meeting on the same subject held at Budheeal, in the Jummoo territory of the Maharajah Gholab Singh, under his son and heir apparent, the Meer Sahib (Prince) Runbheer Singh; on which occasion Mr. Raikes himself was enabled to explain fully to the assembled Rajpoots of the Jummoo and Seealkote districts the measures which had been taken at Mynpooree and Umritsur—

"Quorum pars magna fuit—"

for the suppression of this crime.

So deeply was the author's sympathy enlisted in the

philanthropic movement then going on, that he consented, at the solicitation of a friend, to prepare for an English periodical an account of that meeting, prefaced by a slight sketch of the whole subject. But the work he had thus undertaken, under the impulse of the moment, he found far more difficult than he had at first anticipated. Comparatively ignorant of the social bearings of the subject, and finding himself perpetually at fault in tracing out its history, he realised the truth of the quaint remark of good Bishop Andrewes, that "emptying presupposes filling," and found that if he wished to make the subject intelligible and interesting to others, he must first arrive at a tolerably clear conception of it himself. Thus he was induced to study the subject carefully in all its various phases, and to collect from every available source such information as might be brought to bear on its elucidation. Such spare time as he could command from his more direct clerical duties was devoted to it; and thus was he imperceptibly led on, by the insight (slight though it were) which he was daily gaining into the social system and the history of the Hindoos, until his contemplated "Sketch" assumed such ominous proportions as to make its admission into any periodical quite impossible. By the end of 1854, he had completed what now constitutes the first four chapters of the present work, relating to the measures adopted in Bombay and Rajpootana: but the original subject of which he had undertaken to treat—the Budheeal meeting—was yet in the far distance. The labors of Messrs. Montgomery, Raikes, and Gubbins, at Allahabad, Mynpooree, and Agra, were not yet touched on, much less the great Umritsur meeting, with all the measures of the Punjab Government which had led to and followed it. Therefore, almost in despair of ever accomplishing his task, and feeling how immensely it had already outgrown its original proportions, the author laid the manuscript aside for some months, without, however, letting the subject drop from his mind, or losing any opportunity of collecting materials that came in his way. At the end of the year 1855, the same kind friend who had first suggested the article for a review, and others also who saw the earlier portion of his MS., strongly urged him to continue it, for publication as a separate work; and much encouragement and assistance, to an unlooked-for extent, induced him to persevere, and the following pages are the result.

The sources from which the information has been collected may be here briefly mentioned. The chief authorities on which he has relied for general statements are—Ward on the Hindoos, Elphinstone's and Malcolm's Histories of India, Tod's History of Rajasthan, Colonel Dixon's Mairwarra, Kaye's East India Company's Administration,* &c. He has also largely availed himself of the information given in a very interesting, though rather rhetorical article on the subject, in an early number (No. 2) of the *Calcutta Review*, and a paper of considerable importance on the Bombay Infanticide Fund, in a number (for January, 1841) of the *Oriental Christian Spectator*, published in Bombay; and more recently, while revising the earlier chapters for the press, from a very valuable work, just published, from the pen of Dr. Wilson, on Infanticide in Western India. In every instance, however, where he has quoted from any author, or adopted any ideas on any important point, he has, he believes, acknowledged his obligation by a reference, at the risk of cumbering his pages with foot-notes. These works have been especially referred to in the four earlier chapters.

For the particulars which he has been enabled (for the first time, he believes) to make public, in connexion with the names of Messrs. Thomason and Montgomery, in chapter v., he is wholly indebted to official documents most kindly placed at his disposal by W. Muir, Esq., Secretary to Government of North-Western Provinces, and to information obtained from private sources.

* A work which so fully and fairly treats of its varied subjects as to form a perfect "manual" for the student of Anglo-Indian history.

For the account of the Mynpooree measures, as given in chapter vi., the Notes on the North-Western Provinces, by C. Raikes, Esq., and an article of considerable interest in the Benares Magazine for June, 1852, have been chiefly consulted.

The system adopted by Mr. Gubbins at Agra, as explained in chapter vii., has been collected entirely from the published reports of that energetic officer, contained in No. 15 of the Selections of Correspondence of the North-Western Provinces.

The particulars of the Punjab infanticidal races, given in chapter viii., and continued in the subsequent chapters, the author has gleaned from various quarters; such as Cunningham's, McGregor's, and Prinsep's Histories of the Sikhs, Sir H. Lawrence's Adventurer in the Punjab, Major Edwardes's Twelve Months on the Punjab Frontier, and similar works; and also from two numbers (Vol. i., No. 6, and Vol. ii., No. 9) of the published Selections from the Public Correspondence of the Punjab Government; and scarcely less valuable information has been obtained from unpublished reports from District Officers in the Punjab, besides those included in these Selections, which have been most obligingly laid before him by Mr. Montgomery, the Judicial Commissioner for the Punjab, and Mr. Raikes, the Lahore Commissioner, the two leaders of this movement.

For the statistics, given in chapter xii., he is indebted greatly to the same official sources, and also to many valuable private local communications.

Having thus cursorily enumerated the various sources from which he has obtained the information he has endeavoured in the following pages to give in a digested form, it only remains for him to offer his most grateful acknowledgments to those kind friends through whom it has been obtained. He feels that he has trespassed so much on private friendship, and on the courtesy of even personal strangers (with whom a common interest in the subject furnished sufficient grounds for asking and giving assistance), that it would be impossible to name all to whom he is under obligation.

In now tendering to them, one and all, his grateful thanks for that valuable aid to which his humble production owes so much, he would fain express his earnest hope that they will not consider as altogether misplaced and unprofitable the trouble they have taken, and the kindly interest they have evinced, in the work he has had in hand.

A few words are due also to those whose sympathies he would desire to enlist in a movement now steadily progressing in this remote part of our vast empire. To give anything of a popular character to a subject which so little admitted of departure from historical references and dry details was, as he well knew, very difficult—far too difficult for him to accomplish. But if he has been enabled, by a plain and truthful statement of the motives from which so unnatural a crime is believed to have sprung, and of the measures which have been taken for its suppression, to present it even in a readable form, his end has been accomplished. He is conscious of many faults of composition, and much inornateness of style; but he has done his best to compensate for these by the information he has collected. He would throw himself on the indulgence of his readers, with the assurance that anything approaching to literary merit he has not aimed at; he has only sought (and hopes he has not wholly failed), by some painstaking research, to present a faithful view of a great philanthropic movement, undertaken by Christian rulers for their heathen dependents; and he trusts the imperfections of the work will not tend to the disparagement or depreciation of the subject itself.*

Placed by the great Head of the Church, in whose hands are our times and our places, too, among a people of whom comparatively little is known, in the midst of races in whose internal economy but little interest has

* For the system of spelling Indian words (or, perhaps, absence of all system), he feels how sadly he has exposed himself to the unfavorable criticism of the champions of orthography. He has endeavoured to act on this one principle throughout—namely, of presenting Indian names and words in their most familiar forms, so that, whether rightly or wrongly spelt, they might be most easily recognised.

been felt hitherto by the great majority of English readers, it has afforded him no ordinary pleasure to employ any leisure time from his more direct ministerial duties in studying their history, and examining their habits of life; and he hopes that his present endeavour to throw such light as he could on this dark side of the picture of their social system will not be regarded as time or labor misapplied. Little will he regret either the time or the labor thus happily spent, if he shall be thereby instrumental in arousing the interest and kindling the zeal of a single fellow-countryman, either here or at home, in furtherance of this righteous cause.

Punjab, June, 1856.

CONTENTS.

CHAPTER I.

INDIAN INFANTICIDE: ITS CHARACTER AND MOTIVES.

CHAPTER II.

EARLY EFFORTS FOR ITS SUPPRESSION.

CHAPTER VI.

EFFORTS IN MYNPOOREE.

CHAPTER VII.

EFFORTS IN THE AGRA DISTRICTS.

CHAPTER VIII.

THE PUNJAB: ITS INFANTICIDAL RACES.

CHAPTER IX.

MEASURES RESULTING IN THE UMRITSUR MEETING.

CHAPTER X.

REFLECTIONS ON THE UMRITSUR MEETING.

CHAPTER XI.

SUBSIDIARY DISTRICT MEETINGS.

CHAPTER XII.

STATISTICS OF FEMALE INFANTICIDE.

INDIAN INFANTICIDE.

CHAPTER I.

INDIAN INFANTICIDE: ITS CHARACTER AND MOTIVES.

Infanticide unnatural, yet a world-wide crime—Various motives in different countries—In India pride of caste and exorbitant marriage expenditure lead to the destruction of female infants—General modes of destruction; poison, violence, or neglect—Most prevalent among Rajpoots—Various traditions in its defence—The fancied duty of marrying daughters into higher castes or clans at the root of the crime—Pride thus engendered and cherished, and display encouraged—Bhâts and Chârans chief promoters of extravagance at marriages; account of their office and character—Fear of them universal and intense—Ovid evidently alludes to the crime—Comparison between Indian and English infanticide.

THE affection of a parent for its offspring is the prompting of nature; in the brute beast it is implanted instinctively, and for its time cherished intensely; in man it assumes the purer, loftier character imparted both by reason and revelation, and is hallowed as the type, however feeble and imperfect, of the love borne by the Eternal for His children.

How humiliating, then, is the conviction which history forces upon us, that, with the failure of true religion and the decline of morality, this well-spring, from whence still flowed in mercy a stream of solace and joy, began to dry up in men's hearts! In heathenism men came to be "without natural affection" (αστοργοι, Rom. i. 31). Parental love might still bloom, as one of those "few flowerets of Eden," which fallen man was permitted to inherit, but even on its fair petals "the trail of the serpent" soon appeared, and thus infanticide became "a world-wide crime."

For such it has become. In every quarter of the globe, in the Old World and the New, in countries the most remote from each other, among independent races and people that could have had no mutual intercourse, in every stage, too, of national progress, among the civilised and refined as well as the rude and barbarous, it has been found to exist. In China and North America, in Arabia and New Zealand, amid the highways of classic Greece and the Zenanas of Hindostan, has it reared its hateful form, and made for itself a home. Few are the regions on earth's fair surface but could furnish records of deeds scarcely less revolting than those of which inspiration has graven its indelible impress on "the valley of Hinnom."

The voice of authority has been loudly raised in its condemnation. Confutsee among his brother Celestials, Mahomed among the children of the desert, the code of Justinian and the Shastras, have all reprobated and forbidden it. Greece indeed,

"Mother of arts and arms, immortal Greece,"

stands alone among the nations as having thrown the

cloak of legal sanction over its perpetration.* Yet, excepting those only of Celtic origin (to their honor be it remembered), there is scarcely a people among whom it has not received a tacit recognition.

The motives, however, which have produced it, appear to have been, as might naturally be expected, as diverse as the habits and characters of the nations themselves. The grossest superstition led the worshippers of Moloch to "give their first-born for their transgression, the fruit of their body for the sin of their soul." Pride of manly vigor doubtless prompted the wild rover of the "forest primeval" and the Polynesian savage, as it did the stern Spartan of old, to destroy the infant that betrayed signs of weakness or defect. But among the Hindoos we find other motives, peculiar to themselves, closely and deeply interwoven with their social, or so-called religious system. In India, to use the language of Bishop Heber,† "pride, poverty, and avarice are in league with superstition to perpetuate these horrors." These motives may at first sight appear to be nearly akin to those which influenced both the Canaanite and the Spartan; but they are in reality perfectly distinct. The valley of Hinnom received the blood of children offered in vicarious sacrifice to avert either national calamity or domestic trouble; but those infants whose case we are about to consider, are the victims of a superstition which is at variance with itself,‡ and of a pride, not like the Spartan's, of personal prowess,

* The laws of Lycurgus admitted, if they did not order, the exposure, to almost certain death, of all infants that were sickly or deformed. Beza thinks that St. Paul (Romans i. 31) had especial reference to this in pronouncing want of natural affection as one of the excesses of heathenism.

† Journal, ch. xxiv.

‡ See Appendix.

but of hereditary rank. It is true that at the time when Bishop Heber wrote, there still existed the remains of a form of infanticide not wholly different in character from that of which the Amorite was guilty. At that day infants were still wont to be launched on the stream as votive or propitiatory offerings to the δαιμονες of the sacred rivers of Bengal. But since then the arm of the law has been successfully put forth to arrest the progress of this dreadful fanaticism; and the waters of the Hooglee, the Ganges, and the Jumna, now roll on their fertilising way unrippled by the throes, uncrimsoned by the blood of such victims.

Yet it is to be feared that hundreds and thousands of infants have yearly perished (and are still perishing) in India, for whom English law and English influence sought in vain to provide a way of escape. They were beyond the reach of that merciful law which had rescued so many from a watery grave, which had held back the Hindoo widow from sacrificing herself on her husband's pyre, and had restrained the suicidal votary of Juggernath madly thinking to pass into paradise under the chariot-wheels of his god. In these cases, English rule could vindicate and support the claims of humanity, and check the celebration of such unnatural and unhallowed rites, for they were overt acts, requiring much of preparation, and attended with considerable display; but on the cold-blooded infanticide which is now the bane of India —the destruction of female children at the moment of their birth—what could it effect? It was worse than powerless; for its attempted intervention only drove the perpetrators of this "child murder" into a deeper privacy, and to the use of means of destruction more subtle and secret. The sacred precincts of the Zenana became more closely secured and guarded; and here "pride, poverty, and avarice" (no longer even sanctioned by, or pretending to a league with, superstition) reigned still, in defiance of all laws human and divine, triumphing over and trampling down the heaven-born feeling of parental love, nature's chief connecting link between fallen man and his Divine original!

Before passing on to examine these motives in detail, let us for a moment lift aside the purda* which screens from public gaze the Zenana of the Hindoo, and reveals some of the secrets of that prison-house. Let us suppose the birth of a daughter announced to the father—by a look rather than a word—he is still the parent, and nature's voice is not wholly silenced; let the babe live but one short hour, and nature will claim her own. But no—regret and grief are visible in his face; he does not trust himself to speak; he gives a sign too easily understood, and leaves the rest to his domestics; "it is the affair of the women." Perhaps he is at the moment seeking to soothe his feelings with his hookah and its condiment of bang;† if so, his fingers quickly mould a portion of it into the form of a pill, which he gives in silence to an attendant; this is immediately placed in the roof of the infant's mouth, where it becomes softened by the saliva, and flows with it down the throat, soon throwing the poor babe into its first, and last, long sleep.

* The purda is a thick padded curtain which separates one room from another, and supplies the place of a door.

† An intoxicating decoction from flax or hemp, mixed by Hindoos with their tobacco for smoking.

If this be not at hand, the mother's breast is smeared with a preparation of the juice of the datura (*Datura Alba*), or the Mudar plant (*Asclepias Gigantea*), or the poppy, and the infant drinks in a deadly poison with its first draught of milk. It is said, that among some of the Rajpoot tribes it is customary to dig a hole and fill it with milk, and place the new-born babe in it, when she is quickly drowned. Some, again, dispense with the milk, and actually bury their infants alive! Not unfrequently, before even the infant has an independent existence, the umbilical cord is drawn tightly round the throat, and the child is strangled at its first gasp! These are believed to be the usual modes by which infants are destroyed; and, revolting as it is to contemplate, it is often the mother's hand which, as it were, severs the frail thread of life so lately drawn from herself!

This unnatural crime, though not confined exclusively to any one particular class, is proved to exist especially among the Rajpoots, of which race it will be necessary to speak at some length. But, before doing so, it may be well to premise, for the information of any un-Indian reader who may honor these pages with a perusal, that the Hindoos are divided into four grand orders, or castes, called Brahmans, Kshutreeas, Vaiseeas, and Soodras; representing respectively the priestly, military, mercantile, and laboring classes.* These are again subdivided into innumerable tribes and ramifications of

* Such is the original classification of the Hindoos; the theory is still retained, though practically it ceases to exist. For instance, our soldiers (Sepahees), especially in Bombay, are taken out of all classes indiscriminately, and men of any caste, even Brahmans, will become domestic servants.

tribes, utterly incomprehensible to the uninitiated, but defined among themselves most accurately, and preserved with great jealousy. Of these the Rajpoots hold the highest place under the military order of the Kshutreeas, claiming to be second only to the Brahmans in dignity and sacredness. In common with the other early invaders of India, they are believed to have had their origin amid the heights of the Indian Caucasus (Hindoo Coosh), and like the barbarian invaders of Europe during the fourth and fifth centuries, to have left their mountain homes in quest of plunder, or hope of settlement, in the more fertile and peaceful plains of Hindostan. The tide of conquest and the vicissitudes of war have scattered them over all the northern and western parts of this vast peninsula. They are to be found, in greater or less numbers, from the Sutlej to the Nerbudda, the Jumna, and the Ganges; but their chief stronghold is in the independent states of Ajmere, Jyepore, Odeypore, Malwa, and the minor ones which compose that large district between the Nerbudda and Scinde, called from them "Rajpootana," or "Rajasthan." Among this race, wherever located, infanticide prevails. Yet there are circumstances in the early history of this people which render the perpetration of the crime at their hands the more atrocious; because, as we shall see presently, the very motives which prompt them to it should have been their greatest security against it. They glory in being descended from men who erst headed the warrior tribes of India, who won for themselves renown on some of her greatest battle-fields against Mahmoud of Ghuznee and Tamerlane; who, if their own chroniclers may be believed, performed deeds of high prowess and chivalry that would bear comparison with those of the lion-hearted Richard, the royal Bruce, or the Chevalier Bayard. Who could imagine that such a race, in their pride of high birth and chivalrous descent, could have become so degraded as to think that their ancestral superiority could only be asserted and maintained by resorting to a practice from which those ancestors would have shrunk? Yet so it is; the high-born Rajpoot, of whatever clan, Chohan, Rahtore, Jarejah, or Kutoch, stains the proud escutcheon of his once brave and chivalrous race with the life-blood of his daughter, lest that blood, of such vaunted purity, should flow into meaner veins, or she remain unmarried, and therefore, as he thinks, dishonored!

So universal is this practice among them, that it is clear they must be prompted by one common motive, and what that real motive is we shall see; but it is remarkable that each tribe, by preserving some tradition of its own in exculpation, endeavours to keep *that motive* out of sight, as if ashamed to acknowledge it. One, for instance, traces it to a prophecy delivered by a Brahman to a Rajpoot king, that his race would lose the sovereignty through one of his female posterity; and states that the king, to guard himself and his family against the possible fulfilment of this prophecy, ordered all the female infants of his house to be thenceforward destroyed.*

The Jarejahs of Guzerat, again, tell that one of their Rajahs, having a daughter of unwonted beauty, and

* Ward's Hindoos, part iii. chap. iv. sect. 32.

being unable to find a fitting husband for one of such high rank and loveliness, at the urgent advice of his family priest, put her to death, to avoid the disgrace of her remaining unmarried; and enjoined the duty on all Jarejahs that they should destroy all their female children for ever.* The Chohans of the Doab, on the other hand, have a tradition that one of their princes being sorely pressed by his son-in-law, and smarting under the sense of disgrace which his mere position as the father of a married daughter seemed to entail on him, called together his sons, and bound them by an oath to save his family from future contempt by destroying every female that might be born to them.† A somewhat similar tradition is, according to Major H. Edwardes, advanced by a tribe of Khutrees, called Bedees, of whom more hereafter. Thus it is clear that there is one common motive which they blush to own, and which they try to keep out of sight by putting forth the plea of some hereditary obligation.

It is now time to inquire what can be the real motive which influences so numerous and yet so widely-scattered a race in the perpetration of so unnatural a crime. The first motive, doubtless, is pride of caste; and it operated thus throughout the whole of the Hindoo nation. It is an established custom that a female may not marry into any caste or tribe which is not at least of equal rank with her own. To marry an inferior is, in their eyes, a degradation; but to remain unmarried is actual dishonor.

* Colonel Walker, quoted in Kaye's Administration of the East India Company, p. 552.

† Raikes's Notes on the North-West Provinces, p. 8.

Not believing in the existence of female virtue, they regard marriage as a woman's only safeguard against shame and infamy. Thus a daughter becomes, from the very first, a source of great anxiety to the Hindoo. He cannot allow her to pass even the early years of childhood unbetrothed, or to attain the first stage of puberty unmarried, without incurring the risk of grievous dishonor. One of his first cares, then, must be to provide a fitting husband for her; and his selection must be made from another tribe, or another division of his own tribe, of at least equal, and, if possible, superior rank to his own. It is clear that this very selection affects his pride of caste; it involves an admission of the equality, if not superiority of, perhaps, a rival tribe or clan. Nor is this all: not only is his pride of caste thus wounded, but he has to submit to a personal degradation far greater, and that too of life-long duration. From the day of his daughter's marriage, when on bended knee he presents her to the husband of his choice, prays him to accept her, and even pays him "almost divine honors,"* from that day he becomes subject to his son-in-law, and is in every way treated by him as an inferior. Indeed, to such an extent is this carried, so thoroughly does the Hindoo, as the father of a married daughter, sink in the social scale, that the very title "father-in-law" (Soosur) is used as a common term of scorn and reproach. This position the proud Hindoo foresees, and resolves, if possible, to avoid. Rather than submit either to the humiliation of seeking for a husband worthy of his daughter, and the indignities which her

* See Ward on the Hindoos, part iii. chap. iv. sect. 32.

marriage would subject him to, or to the still more dreaded alternative of seeing her remain unmarried, and, as he thinks, dishonored, he destroys her at her birth. So deplorably false is his code of morals, that he is led to regard the murder of his own child as preferable to the risk of losing caste or honor.

The natural result of this principle will be that the higher the caste or tribe the more frequent will be the crime; the higher born the Hindoo, as a general rule, the more proud is he of his birth, and the more sensitively alive to the preservation of his dignity; both of which would be so seriously affected, as he thinks, by having to provide a husband for a daughter. And statistical research most fully confirms this: every step we ascend up this ladder of castes* we find females become fewer and fewer, till on reaching the top they altogether disappear. So glaring is the disproportion between the sexes, among the high caste Hindoos, that the most casual observer cannot fail to be struck by it; and the fact of such a disparity has often been urged in confirmation of the suspicion that they did not suffer their girls to live. But such an admission can very rarely be extorted from them; generally speaking, they vehemently repudiate the imputation; and the explanation which they offer is one in which it is difficult to decide whether blasphemy or absurdity preponderates. They profess to ascribe it to the "will of Heaven" marking them out in their "pride of place" as objects of its especial favor by giving them only sons!

* This does not apply to Brahmans, who are believed to be generally innocent of this crime.

Pride, then—the pride of birth—engendered and made hereditary by the very nature of the Hindoo social system, may be justly regarded as the primary motive to infanticide. But there is also another motive, scarcely less powerful, and one from the influence of which no caste or tribe is altogether free, and the existence and extent of which was not, we venture to think, sufficiently recognised in the earlier attempts which were made to suppress the crime, to which it so materially contributed: it is poverty—that poverty which results from the exorbitant expenditure which prevails among them at the marriage of their daughters. It is easy to trace the connexion between these two motives, and to see how the latter had its origin in the former. Pride of high birth tempted to display, at any cost, on such occasions, until such extravagant display grew to be regarded as essential to, and indeed as proof of, high birth.

It has been remarked that universal custom requires the Hindoo to select for his daughter a husband of some tribe or grade equal to, and, if possible, higher than his own; and the bridegroom elect requires to be paid in proportion to his dignity and condescension. Now, this is a principle not altogether unknown in England. What wealthy cit—for records of whose ancestral greatness the archives of the Heralds' College would be ransacked in vain—would ever dream of the possibility of seeing the fair brows of a daughter, however lovely and accomplished, encircled with a coronet, unless he were prepared to throw a goodly dower into the matrimonial scales, as a counterpoise to the rank and title of his noble son-in-law? Nor is it held "on 'Change," or in Lombard-street, that a man must necessarily be a *Sir Giles Overreach* because his chief delight in amassing his wealth may have lain (and he the while not blush to confess it), like that worthy's, in the fond hope and thought "to have his daughter 'Right Honorable.'" The principle is sanctioned; but reprobated and condemned only in its exaggerated form and cruel results. In England it is optional; in India compulsory, with the force of law rather than custom. There it is only the millionaire who thinks of bidding so high for a noble son-in-law. The man of moderate means and less ambition is content to bestow his daughter on her equal, so there be only a reasonable prospect of happiness and competence, or to retain her in her home sphere. Here* there is no choice: the Hindoo, if he would escape the imagined degradation of his daughter marrying an inferior, or the disgrace of her remaining unmarried, is compelled to provide a husband for her, and to pay for him too; and that, not according to his own means, but according to the relative rank of his house and that of his son-in-law elect. Nor is the dower (Daega)—enormous though that sometimes is—the half of what he is obliged to spend in contracting the marriage for his daughter. Presents in money, clothes, jewels, sweetmeats, and what not, on at least a score prescribed occasions between the betrothal (Buddun) and the marriage (Shadee), must be made to every one who can claim kith or kin to the bridegroom.

But the crowning triumph of extravagance and imposture is reserved for the marriage-day itself; then the

* In explanation of this and similar expressions, it must be borne in mind that this was written in India.

house of the bride's father is surrounded by a flock of "harpies," as rapacious, and scarcely less loathsome than those foul creations of Virgil's brain. These are known by the name of Bhâts and Chârans. They are to be found in all parts of India, and everywhere unfortunately exercise a baneful influence over all classes of Hindoos. As their connexion with the marriage ceremonies will bring them into frequent notice in the following pages, it may be well in this place to give a slight sketch of their character and occupation.

Mythology assigns to them a somewhat remarkable origin.* Mahadeo had, it is said, a sacred bull, for the purpose of guarding which he first created the race of Bhâts; but he had also a pet lion which was kept in the same place with the bull, and in spite of the noisy efforts of the Bhâts to effect a rescue, the lion used every day to dine off the sacred bull, thereby entailing a great deal of trouble on Siva, to say nothing of the grief it caused him, for he was obliged to create a new bull every day in the room of the one killed by the lion. The Bhâts were consequently degraded from their office, and a new race of men called Chârans were created, who were more courageous than the Bhâts, and more successful guardians of the sacred bull.

What possible resemblance there is between the Bhâts and Chârans of Brahmanical fiction and those of everyday life it is difficult to discover. At present they are a contemptible race, though not altogether without their uses. The Bhâts are the bards or minstrels; and their

* Bishop Heber's Journal, chap. xxiii.

office is held in such great respect, that to kill or to beat one of their order is not only considered disgraceful, but most ominous, if not fatal to the worldly prospects, and even the life, of the perpetrator of the act. The Chârans, too, are bards; but their distinctive character is that of heralds, or genealogists; and their authority as living records of family descent and rights is so high, that they are frequently made the referees in the investigation of rival claims to property. In some parts of India, especially in Guzerat and Rajpootana, the general respect for their office, and their reputed courage, make them the safest guards for the transmission of the most valuable property, in whose custody it is considered sacred. There are few among the wealthy Hindoos who do not retain, as part of their household, a family Bhât or Châran, that on festive occasions their names may be blended with the praises of the gods and heroes chanted by the former, and with the glorious exploits of their ancestors recounted by the latter. And we may be sure these men do their best to make their presence welcome by bestowing a due amount of flattery on their patrons. Such, of course, are of the better sort, though only to prove the more rapacious when occasion offers.* There are others, too, of the lowest class, abounding in the cities and villages, where, claiming a right to be present, and to be paid, at every marriage that may take place, they levy such a tax on the inhabitants as to become a burden and a curse.

The English reader must not, then, picture to himself, as the concomitants of a Hindoo marriage, some venerable

* The Rajah of Odeypore is said to have given a lac of rupees (10,000*l.*) to his chief Bhât on the occasion of a marriage in his family.

harper heading a group of brethren of the lyre, like our friend the "aged Ferrand," with his neighbouring minstrels, who had flocked around him, adding their "tributary lays" to honor the bridal of the "Fair Maid of Lorn."* A more truthful picture he will find in the words of an older poet:

> "Ambubaiarum collegiæ . . . .
> Mendici, mimæ, balatrones, et hoc genus omne."

The Bhâts and Chârans—bards and heralds—alike prostitute their honorable office to the most mercenary ends. They gather together from miles around, like vultures on their prey, bringing with them all the idle and the dissolute, who on such occasions, be they minstrels, dancers, buffoons, barbers, or beggars, all pass for Bhâts and Chârans. Such is the motley group that, under that once honorable but degraded name, flock around the house of the bride's father, demanding "largess," not

> "With symphony, and dance, and song,"

but with a din, and discord, and clamor to which the very "marrow-bones and cleavers" of a band of London butchers' apprentices would be a dulcet harmony. On such a day, not a man, or a woman, or a child, or even a donkey or a dog, but is worth his rupee; and if some luckless giver of the feast be bold enough to resist such extortion, he must do it at the risk of personal indignity and insult, if not actual injury. He must be prepared to have his own name and his daughter's branded with every term of contumely and scorn, instead of being

* See the Lord of the Isles.

lauded as worthy of a high-born race; and to receive jeers and curses in the place of flattery and benisons. Very few men are prepared for this; and, therefore, reluctantly, and with the best grace they may, they succumb to a custom originating in vanity and false ambition—now sanctioned by centuries of usage, and fostered and perpetuated by the dreaded influence of those who batten on the spoil. One such day of reckless extravagance often entails a life-long want, and a debt which that life is all too short to repay, and which thus becomes a heritage of misery to those who come after. The man of substance, perhaps, feels but little the thousands and thousands of rupees which he thus squanders; but the poor man (and India furnishes but few exceptions to the proverbial connexions between high-born pride and poverty)—the poor man, whose daily wages rarely exceed four annas (sixpence), cannot thus, to celebrate his daughter's marriage, scatter to the winds two or three hundred rupees (20*l.* or 30*l.*), his hard-earned, closely-stored savings, or, more frequently, his dearly-effected loan, without rueing the day that his daughter was born.

Under such a system, who can wonder that the Rajpoot, and more or less every Hindoo, "mourns when a daughter is born to him, and rejoices when he has a son? The one brings disgrace, anxiety, or, at the very least, heavy expense upon his house; the other increases his wealth and his dignity."*

Is it possible that Ovid had gained some insight into the character and motives of Hindoo female infanticide?

* Raikes's Notes on the North-West Provinces, p. 9.

The existence of it was certainly known to the Romans of his day; and nothing can accord more exactly with those motives than the language he puts into the mouth of Lygdus when addressing Telethusa, about to become a mother:

> "Marem parias! onerosior altera sors est;
> . . . .
> Edita forte tuo fuerit si fœmina partu
> (Invictus mando, pietas ignosce!) necetur."
>
> MET. lib. ix. l. 675.

To these two motives, then, either separately or in combination—to pride of race and poverty, resulting from exorbitant marriage expenditure—the infanticide now prevalent in India may be generally attributed. Exceptions to this rule, or modifications of it, may be occasionally met with; but, generally speaking, the Hindoo's pride and his purse are sought to be saved by the sacrifice of his child!

It is not our intention, nor would it come within our province in this general review of the subject, to enter into a closer analysis of these two motives. To others, more able or more ethically minded, we will leave the task of testing their relative enormity in the crucible of casuistry. For ourselves, we are content, at the risk of being misunderstood and condemned, to take a somewhat charitable view of both motives, and to judge of this crime at the hands of the Hindoo on the principle so wisely laid down by Sir J. Malcolm in his farewell "Instructions," "by a standard which is suited to their belief, their usages, their habits, their occupations, their rank in life, the ideas they have imbibed in infancy, and the stage of civilisation to which they are advanced."

Deploring most bitterly (and who can fail to do so?) that so dense a veil should be drawn over their moral vision, we consider that it is demanded of our own enlightenment and our Christianity to strive, so far as in us lies, to remove such "scales" of ignorance, to close up the avenues to such influences, and to leave no longer any room for such motives; and to every one who shall take part in so good a work, most heartily do we bid him "God speed."

Nor can we conclude this part of our subject without a passing remark on the form of infanticide which has of late years been so greatly on the increase among our own countrymen. We confess that we almost find some extenuation for the guilt of a Hindoo mother who at her husband's command destroys her infant daughter to save his ancestral pride, or to avert the poverty which her marriage might entail, when contrasted with the atrocity of the mother in Christian England, who stains her hand with the life-blood of a child of unwedded love to remove all trace of her shame, or with that of the wife who brings her offspring to an untimely end to make up a case for charity, or to defraud a "burial club."

CHAPTER II.

EARLY EFFORTS FOR ITS SUPPRESSION.

The Emperor Jehangeer and Rajah Jye Singh — English long ignorant of this form of the crime—Hindoo Zenanas impenetrable—The crime committed secretly — Detection very difficult — Mr. Jonathan Duncan, Resident of Benares, first discovered it among Rajkoomar Rajpoots — Appointed Governor of Bombay—The crime discovered among Jarejahs of Kattyawar, and throughout the Western Coast—Major Alexander Walker, Resident at Baroda, tries to bring Jarejahs to bind themselves to suppress the crime—Difficulties and opposition—Rao of Bhooj defies him—"Covenants" eventually signed—Measures inquisitorial and coercive—Success apparent—Most gratifying proofs of it—Walker departs for England—Duncan dies—Supervision relaxed—Crime revives—Captain Carnac succeeds Colonel Walker at Baroda—Rao of Noanuggur heavily fined—Rao of Murvee honored—Want of vigorous support from Bombay—A period of indifference—The pains and penalties questionable.

SUCH is the form of infanticide which at the present day exists in India, and such the motives from which it springs. Let us now proceed to inquire what efforts have been made to wipe away this blood-stain from the face of this country—a stain as ancient as the days of classic Rome and Greece. Have the native rulers ever exerted themselves to put a stop to a custom of the prevalence of which they could not be ignorant? Or were they themselves too deeply implicated in its perpetration to adopt any hearty and vigorous measures for its suppression? Two persons only are mentioned in history as having made the slightest attempt to effect this—the one a Mahomedan emperor, the other a high Rajpoot prince. Jehangeer, in the beginning of the seventeenth century, having had it brought to his notice that the practice was rife in a village near which he chanced to be travelling, immediately issued a stringent order against it, and threatened to subject to the torture any one who should be thenceforth proved guilty of the crime. The act was worthy of the well-meaning but capricious emperor; and it met with all the success that might have been looked for. It was like a surgeon cauterising a single sore, but taking no steps to arrest the ravages of a disease infecting the whole system. For in the human body and the body politic alike, a local application, however active, cannot be expected to eradicate a constitutional malady. And such was the very natural result of Jehangeer's order. The crime remained unchecked throughout the rest of his empire, and ere long revived again in that particular village with renewed vigor! About a hundred years after, however, a far more prudent and sagacious plan was adopted in Rajpootana itself, by Jye Singh, the Rajah of Jyepore, or Amber. According to Colonel Tod, he "submitted to the Thakoor, or prince, of every Rajpoot state a decree regulating the Daega, or dower, and other marriage expenditure, with reference to the property of the vassal, limiting it to one year's income of the estate: this plan was, however, frustrated by the Chandawat of Saloombra, who expended on the marriage of his daughter a sum even greater than his sovereign could have afforded; and to have his name blazoned by the bards and genealogists he sacrificed the beneficent views of one of the wisest of the Rajpoot race." *

The crime was too firmly rooted, too deeply ingrained into their very natures, to be removed by such partial measures; and, doubtless, feelings of interest and shame held back the native rulers from anything like strenuous combined action; and thus, whatever they did attempt, was done with reluctance and feebly, and necessarily proved futile.

But what, we must go on to ask, has England, with "a power," as Mr. Raikes says, "greater than Eastern nation or emperor ever saw," attempted towards putting down such a miserable practice as this of murdering little children?

It must be admitted that we cannot carry back our review of these attempts to an early period of our settlement in the country. It was not till the end of the last century that the subject appears to have attracted any notice. The period which immediately followed the rescue of Calcutta from the Mahomedan, called forth the warrior spirit alone. During those eventful years of mutual suspicion and secret intrigue, no less than open hostility, while native and European were in league against us, it was enough that England could "hold her own;" and to make her footing sure she was being constantly driven to fresh defensive wars and fresh acquisitions as the result of her victories. Those stirring times

* Tod's Rajasthan, vol. i. p. 637.

of Clive and Warren Hastings gave full occupation to men's minds in the momentous struggles which followed each other in rapid succession, and left but little time or opportunity for acquiring a knowledge of the secret springs—" the inner man"—of the Hindoo system. It were unjust to impute indifference or incapacity to the magistracy of India because they suffered this inhuman practice of infanticide to remain unchecked during the latter half of the last century; for, in good sooth, it may be avowed without shame that its very existence in that form was unknown, or at least the proofs of it were far too vague to admit of its being satisfactorily dealt with. No doubt there were certain very suspicious circumstances occasionally coming before the magistrates; enough to make them feel sure that in some localities, and among some classes, female children must be made away with: but there were no evidences of its perpetration on which it could be brought home to any one, so as to ensure punishment. The best idea of the great difficulties which attended any effort to detect it may be gained from the recorded fact, that at a time when very active measures were being taken for its suppression among the Jarejahs of Western India, there was, during a period of twenty-five years, only *one case* in which investigation resulted in conviction and punishment.* To persons utterly unacquainted with the character or domestic life of the Hindoo, it may perhaps seem that these difficulties are exaggerated, and are not really so insurmountable. But let them only compare the married

* Mr. Willoughby's Report on Infanticide, quoted *post*, pp. 48, 49.

life of the high-caste Hindoo with that of the Englishman. The latter regards his wife as every way his equal; she is the ornament of his house no less than the companion of his hearth. The former regards his as little better than his slave—and at the same time contemplates her with a jealousy so intense, that he never suffers her to be seen uncovered, if seen at all, and so lasting, that it only ceases with the funeral pyre which consumes his own body; indeed, so completely does he try to throw a veil over the existence of the female portion of his family, that he does not suffer the name of wife or daughter (supposing him to be of such low caste as to have any of the latter) to pass his lips. Thus the whole domestic life of the one is as private and secret as that of the other is public and unconstrained. Is it not too true that, with all this openness, this publicity, stamped upon the English home, deeds of blood have been perpetrated there to which no clue was furnished at the time? There are legends, of an age not so very remote from our own, which have cast a shade of mystery over many an old baronial hall, or manor-house, or grange, that did not wholly derive their origin from the romancer's brain: something, at least, of truth they had for a foundation, whatever fiction may have done to rear upon it a superstructure of awe-inspiring interest; truth enough to prove that even in the public homes of Englishmen there had been opportunities and means, and hands ready to use them, for removing out of the way some object of rivalry, jealousy, revenge, or avarice, and yet the perpetrator the while escape punishment, or even suspicion. If this, then, were possible in England

—and that it was possible proofs are now, thou[illegible] tribes, late for justice, occasionally being brought to light—[illegible] is comparatively easy was it for the Hindoo, in the secrecy of his house, screened behind the closely-guarded purda of his Zenana, to elude notice, and to defy investigation! Few are the witnesses when the brief life of some unwelcome daughter has to be destroyed; and their mouths are safely closed by fear or a bribe!

This has ever been found to be the great obstacle in the way of detecting and suppressing infanticide in India. The magistrate might suspect, and feel satisfied in his own mind, that where, in a single town or among a particular class, the streets were crowded with boys of every age and grade, yet not one girl was seen, or ever known to be born, there must have been foul play: but how could he prove it? How prevent it? Let him adopt the most inquisitorial measures, yet what more easy than to evade them? What more easy or more common (as has been since discovered) than to remove the pregnant wife to some safer retreat, into the Alsatia, for instance, of some neighbouring independent Rajah's territory, where, if a son were born, the birth might, on the mother's return, be announced and hailed with all due solemnity and rejoicings, but if a daughter, the event become as though it had never been? Here, then, lay the great difficulty; and although the wisdom and perseverance of able and prudent magistrates has, in some measure, overcome it, still does it exist; and it is not too much to say that, with such a class of men, and such principles of action to contend against, no inquisitorial system, no penal enactments, however stringent, would life of thuually suppress the crime. The magistrate may maron, and search, and threaten to punish to the utmost, the Hindoo father will still find means to evade detection, or keep out of the reach of the law. Would we cut down this upas-tree, which is blighting the happiness and peace of thousands of parents, and destroying tens of thousands of infants, we must strike at its root. To eradicate this hateful crime, we must attack the motives from which it springs.

But it is time to consider what has been attempted by the English during the sixty years that the existence of the practice has been known. In the year 1789, Mr. Jonathan Duncan, a member of the East India Company's civil service, at that time Resident of Benares, first discovered the prevalence of the crime in that neighbourhood among the Rajkoomars, an important tribe of the great Rajpoot family. So interesting a communication—the first, we may well believe, which was ever made, either officially or privately, on that subject—cannot be better given than in his own words. He thus brought the subject to the notice of Government in a letter to Lord Cornwallis, then Governor-General of India, in the close of the year 1789:—"I am well assured," says Mr. Duncan, "and it is, indeed, here generally believed, and being so, it is my duty not to keep such enormities, however sanctioned by usage, from the knowledge of Government, that it is no unfrequent practice among the tribe of Rajkoomar to destroy their daughters by causing their mothers to refuse them nurture; whence this race of men do often, from necessity, marry into other Rajpoot families. . . . . This horrid custom is said to exist also among some other tribes, more especially in the Vizier's* dominions; and it is thought to be founded in the extravagant desire of independence entertained by this race of men, joined, perhaps, to the supposed necessity of procuring a suitable settlement in marriage for those devoted females were they allowed to grow up, and the disgrace which would ensue from any omission in that respect. Nor is this species of atrocity of recent institution; for a similar prejudice, as existing among the Indians, was known among the ancient Greeks and Romans, as is found in the relations they have left of this quarter of the globe."† Such was the official announcement made by Mr. Duncan. The existence of the crime obtained greater publicity through Sir John Shore (afterwards Lord Teignmouth), who, as the President of the Asiatic Society, laid the subject before that body in the year 1794. The very language which he used on that occasion shows that he felt he was bringing forward a fact hitherto unknown; and though addressing the *savans* of India—the men who of all others had made the history, religion, and customs of the Hindoos the subject of special research—yet he thought it necessary to preface his announcement of the prevalence of a crime of such unwonted atrocity with some remarks to anticipate and remove their probable doubts and incredulity. He, too, shall speak for himself: "That the practice of infanticide should ever be so general as to become a custom with any sect or race of

* Kingdom of Oude.
† Cited in Kaye's Administration of the East India Company, p. 555.

people requires the most unexceptional evidence to gain belief; and I am sorry to say that the general practice, as far as regards female infants, is fully substantiated with respect to a particular tribe on the frontier of Joudpore, a district in the province of Benares, adjoining to the country of Oude. A race of Hindoos, called Rajkoomars, reside here; and it was discovered in 1789 only that the custom of putting to death their female offspring had long subsisted, and did actually then very much prevail among them. The Resident of Benares (Mr. Duncan), in a circuit which he made through the country where the Rajkoomars dwell, had an opportunity of authenticating the existence of the custom from their own confessions : he conversed with several : all unequivocally admitted it, though all did not fully acknowledge its atrocity."

Having made this astounding discovery, Mr. Duncan did not content himself with reporting it officially to Government, as if thereby absolved of all further personal concern; he applied himself sedulously to devise some plan by which it might be checked; and no sooner had he succeeded in forming such a plan, than he at once began to put it in force. In Duncan's plan was much which a deeper insight into the Hindoo "polity" would lead men to look upon as crude and imperfect. His error chiefly lay in too high an opinion of the Hindoo character for integrity and truthfulness. On this rock he made shipwreck of his hopes. But shall we, in consequence, detract from the high praise due to him who first came forward to face so heinous a practice?

Such was Mr. Duncan's course; he assembled the Rajkoomar chiefs, reasoned with them, and obtained from them a solemn "covenant" that they would renounce the practice. He also suggested a plan for bribing them, as it were, to abandon it; he proposed to Government that pecuniary rewards should be offered for all females that might be born and reared. This, however, did not meet with the approval of the Court of Directors; and "no wonder," as Mr. Raikes justly observes, "lest good men who killed no daughters and got no dowers might be tempted to imitate the Rajpoots' example."* Instead of acting as a check, it would have been setting a premium on this child-murder.

The benevolent efforts of Mr. Duncan appear to have been at first attended with some amount of success: but this proved to be very short-lived; the Rajkoomars soon broke the "covenant" into which they had entered with so much apparent readiness, and were quickly perpetrating the crime as frequently and systematically as ever.

One great cause of this was probably the short period during which Mr. Duncan was able to put his measures to the test. He could do little more than initiate them; he could not personally superintend and watch their working, and modify or alter them as experience might suggest. In the end of 1795, within a year of Sir John Shore's announcement to the Asiatic Society, Mr. Duncan was removed from the Residency at Benares to the more honorable post of Governor of Bombay.

* Notes on North-West Provinces, p. 15.

Here, as we shall see, he found a far wider field for the exercise of his philanthropy, and in the Resident at the Court of Baroda, Major Alexander Walker, a most ready and able coadjutor.

Baroda is the capital of an extensive territory lying north of the Nerbudda, along the Bay of Cambay, and including a considerable portion of the peninsula of Guzerat; it is under a Mahratta prince, generally known by the family name of the Guicowar, who exercises an independent rule, but is, at the same time, tributary to the English, and has always at his Court an English representative. Baroda is a city of considerable antiquity, and of no little repute under the old Rajpoot reign and during the Mahomedan invasions; but its former fame has been well-nigh forgotten in the more recent notoriety for chicanery and corruption which that Court has obtained in connexion with the name of the dauntless Outram,* the late Resident there. It was at this Court that, about half a century before, Major Alexander Walker was Resident, when Mr. Duncan was Governor of Bombay; and in him did Mr. Duncan, who at Benares had stood forth almost single-handed and alone to fight the good fight of humanity, find a kindred spirit, one scarcely inferior to himself in benevolence, zeal, and energy, and ready to co-operate with him fully in the noble cause he had so much at heart.

How great need he had of such sympathising aid we may judge when we consider the rampant form infanticide had assumed along the western shores of Hindostan.

* General Outram, now Chief Commissioner of Oude. This gallant officer was happily described by Sir Charles Napier as "the Bayard of the East."

Mr. Duncan had hitherto seen it only in a single tribe, and that not a very extensive one, of Rajkoomar Rajpoots; but here reports of its prevalence crowded in upon him from every quarter. In Surat, in Cutch, in Guzerat, and still more in Joudpore, and the several states of Rajpootana, it existed as a regular system. Here was the very stronghold of infanticide; and here these two good men and true, Duncan* and Walker, were prepared to throw themselves into the breach, if by so doing they might but carry it by storm. Many and urgent as were the calls upon them in the discharge of their political duties, regulating troubled Courts in troublous times, thwarting French intrigues, and arbitrating between rival native powers, they still found time to listen to other calls which were made upon them as men and Christians.

In the neighbourhood of Baroda, and more or less along the whole of the western coast, there was a numerous and powerful clan, calling themselves Rajpoots, under the title of Jarejahs, among whom infanticide was found to be universally practised. This tribe, according to their own traditions, claimed to be among the highest and purest

* However short-lived the success of his anti-infanticidal measures may have been, in other matters his fame has long survived him, as is testified by a very recent traveller over this field of his earlier labors. The "Bird's-eye View of India," with its appended Journal, by Sir Erskine Perry, which has appeared while these sheets were passing through the press, contains the following most gratifying testimony to the freshness of his remembrance: "I was pleased to find, whilst at Benares, in what grateful recollection the names of Warren Hastings and Jonathan Duncan, and particularly the latter, were held by the inhabitants. Jonathan Duncan, who was afterwards Governor of Bombay, originally *settled* Benares, as the expression is, and his institutions have had the singular fortune, so rare in India, of subsisting intact to this day. A common form of speech by a native of Benares, who desires to say something flattering to a European, is, 'I your slave,—you my god, my father and mother, my *Dunkin*.'" — Chap. xxxviii. p. 229.

branches of the great Rajpoot family; but Colonel Tod, the historian of Rajasthan, assigns to them a far less honorable place in that genealogical tree. He says that it is currently reported among the neighbouring tribes that the Jarejahs had at one time renounced their Hindooism and become Mahomedans; but were never cordially received and trusted by the followers of the Prophet, and were before long altogether cast off by them. This imputation of apostasy they, of course, loudly deny; yet, whatever be the cause, this whole tribe is held in contempt by Hindoo and Mahomedan alike. Indeed, so utterly are they despised by the pure Rajpoot families around, that, to use the words of Colonel Tod, "the owner of a hide of land (Seesodea, Rahtore, or Chohan)" —that is, the pettiest landholder among those high clans— "would spurn the hand of a Jarejah princess." Among these Jarejah subjects of the Guicowar, infanticide was universal; and here, too, pride of birth was the evil genius of their house; whether it were with the fond hope of sustaining its questioned integrity, or with the idea of being avenged on the neighbouring tribes for their calumnies, not a daughter lived to ennoble a rival clan, or to peril the honor of her own.

Major Walker at once saw the difficulty of throwing down such a barrier of pride as here presented itself. In his first communication with the Bombay Government he expressed himself as not being very sanguine as to the result. At the outset he avowed his fears that "the humane attempt" of the Bombay Government would "not be successful to any great extent in restraining the superstitions and religious prejudices of a tribe so far removed from the authority of the British Government, and so little acquainted with the principles of improved society." At a later period, after a further intercourse with the tribe, he declared his conviction that "sentiments of nature and humanity had no influence with the Jarejahs." How fully justified he was in forming so low an estimate of their character in this particular needs no stronger proof than that which is given in a letter he received from one of their leading chieftains, the Rao (or Prince) of Bhooj, the modern capital of Cutch. This letter is given in "Moor's Hindoo Infanticide," and is quoted in "Wallace's Memoirs of India."* It is so remarkable for its tone—distinctly avowing the practice, and defying the English to interfere with it at their peril—as to deserve insertion. "It is notorious," he says, "that since the Awatar of Shri Krishna, the Jarejahs, who are descended from the Hindoos, have, during a period of 4900 years, been accustomed to kill their daughters; and it has no doubt come to your knowledge that of all God's creation, even the mighty Emperors of Hindostan, besides all others the conductors of the affairs of this world, have preserved friendship with this Court, and never acted in this respect unreasonably. But you, who are an Amir of the great Sircar (the Honorable Company), having written to me on this subject, I have felt much uneasiness, for it does not accord with your good character. This Durbar has always maintained friendship with the Honorable Company; and, notwithstanding this, you have acted so un-

* This letter is quoted by Wallace as a continuous whole, and so it is given above; but from Dr. Wilson's work on "Infanticide in Western India," it appears not to be the whole letter, but a selection only of the more striking portions of it.

reasonably in this respect that I am much distressed. No one has until this day wantonly quarrelled with this Court who has not in the end suffered loss. Do not again address me on this subject."*

This letter will suffice to show how deeply rooted were the prejudices he had arrayed against him. Yet, in the face of this defiant form which was assumed by the Jarejahs; in the face, too, of calculations† which even on the most moderate scale displayed an appalling prevalence of the crime, Walker labored on to perform, if it were possible, the task he had undertaken. He, no doubt, felt what was expressed by one who some years after succeeded him as political agent at Kattyawar (Mr. Willoughby, of the Bombay civil service), that "it was not to be expected that a whole tribe would at once relinquish a custom in which, however barbarous, they rather prided

* To this may be added extracts from two other letters of the same character:

Letter from the Jarejah Jehajee of Murvee to Colonel Walker.

Sept. 24, 1807.

"Your letter, Sir, I have received, in which it is written to rear up and protect our daughters; but the circumstances of this case are, that from time immemorial the Jarejahs have never reared their daughters, nor can it now be the case."

From the Mother of Jehajee to Colonel Walker.

Sept. 24, 1807.

"Your letter has been received, and its contents understood. You have called upon Koer Jehajee to rear up his daughters; but it is so, that for many years past none of the Jarejah tribes have ever reared their female offspring. Further particulars of this concern you will learn from Koer Jehajee's writing; and you must excuse him on this score."—See No. 13, referred to in Colonel Walker's Report.

"Within twelve months of the date of the foregoing letters" (says Dr. Buchanan, in his "Christian Researches," p. 52), "Jarejah Jehajee himself, Jehajee's mother, and Futteh Mahomed, formally abjured the practice of infanticide, and were soon followed by the Jarejah tribes in general."

† Some statistical returns led to the belief that of female infants destroyed yearly by this single tribe of Jarejahs, there could not be less than twenty or thirty thousand; and even Major Walker, willing to take the lowest estimate, was prepared to believe that not less than from three to four thousand helpless innocents were thus sacrificed every year to this demon spirit by this tribe alone.

themselves, instead of regarding it as an indelible stain on their character." Yet neither discouragement nor repulse made him desist. As he had not been sanguine of speedy success at the commencement, so neither did he despair when he found success still far off. He appealed again and again to the chiefs of the tribe. He pointed out how grievously this practice violated the laws of nature; how repugnant it was to the feelings of all civilised nations, and especially so to that nation which was then the paramount power in Hindostan. Thus at length his arguments and persuasions began to tell. After some time he succeeded in winning over many of the Jarejah chiefs to bind themselves by an agreement, even more stringent than that made by the Rajkoomars in Bengal; and whereas, before his exertions, "only five instances were known where parental feelings had overcome the general custom of the tribe,"* he was able to announce to Government that within ten months of his obtaining the promises of the Jarejah chiefs there were thirty-two female infants preserved. A few years after, Rajpootnee mothers might be seen bringing their little girls to Major Walker's tent, and presenting them to him with every mark of genuine gratitude and maternal affection, and calling them his children.†

And, to use the words of Bishop Heber,‡ "previous to his" (Colonel Walker's) "departure from Guzerat he received the most affecting compliment which a good man could receive, in being welcomed at the gate of the palace, on some public occasion, by a procession of girls of high

* Mr. Willoughby's Report. † Wallace's Memoirs of India, p. 399.
‡ Journal, chap. xxiv.

rank, who owed their lives to him, and who came to kiss his clothes and throw wreaths of flowers over him as their deliverer and second father."*

Nor did the humane labors of this truly good man, and no less valuable public servant, cease on his withdrawal from India. In the retirement of his English home they, among whom so many of the best years of his life had been spent, and to whose amelioration the noblest energies of his mind had been devoted, still occupied a prominent place in his thoughts. He laid before the Court of Directors at some length, and in the most forcible language, the principles on which he believed the "holy war" against this barbarous and unnatural custom could be best carried on, explaining fully the motives as well as the objects of all the measures he had been instrumental in introducing in the Western Presidency.

It was, however, his misfortune to learn that the system he had so sedulously labored to organise had been little appreciated, and his own labors and motives misrepresented and misunderstood. A few years only after he had retired from the service, while loud pæans were being sounded on the supposed suppression of the crime —while the tomb of his patron and fellow-laborer, now no more, testified to the general belief that "infanticide"

* Since the above was written, the "Infanticide of Western India," by Dr. Wilson, has been published, and from it the following passage is extracted, as containing a touching reference to what was probably the same event as that alluded to by Bishop Heber: "How affecting it must have been for him" (Colonel Walker) "to hear, as he actually did at Dharoal, the tender Rajpoot daughter, rescued from the murderous hand of the parental destroyer, exclaim with infantile voice, 'Colonel Walker saved me!' This must have been more precious to his generous heart than even the approbation of his country."—Page 92.

was "abolished in Kattyawar"*—it was found that the practice had been revived in almost all its former frequency; that, regardless of the solemn covenant into which they had entered, the Jarejahs had relapsed into their old daughter-slaying atrocities; and that the flame was only burning all the more brightly and fiercely for the water which had been for a time thrown upon it. Nor was this all. It was not enough that he thus learned their short-lived success; the failure of measures into which he had thrown his whole soul were attributed to himself, or rather it was insinuated officially by the Bombay Government that his influence and exertions had been over-estimated, and the reports of their original success had been inaccurate! It was easy for Walker to justify himself against such a charge; easy to show, as he did in a most powerful communication to the Court of Directors in 1819, that, by their own admissions, the blame rested on the Government of Bombay; on the apathy and remissness of the local officials, who had failed to require what he had so strongly urged the necessity of—regular returns of births among the suspected families, by which means the increase or decrease of the crime might have been constantly watched; and the very consciousness of such vigilance would have acted as a check on the Jarejahs themselves. Thus the shaft of calumny hurled at him fell harmless, beyond the grief which it caused to his own generous heart. These unjust insinuations he well knew were no echoes from the India House. The Court of Directors had

* On Mr. Jonathan Duncan's tomb in Bombay Cathedral these words are inscribed—"Infanticide abolished in Benares and Kattyawar."

more than once declared their approval and appreciation of his philanthropic zeal; and, shortly after, they still more publicly and substantially recognised his services in India by appointing him Governor of St. Helena.*

But to resume our narrative. Colonel Walker had been succeeded in the Residency of Baroda by Captain Carnac, of the Bombay army, who had previously been his assistant at that Court, and had imbibed no small portion of his anti-infanticidal zeal. With a determination and perseverance, from the consequences of which the Bombay Government, now no longer backed by the energy and vigor of Duncan, seemed to have shrunk, Captain Carnac, in 1811, insisted on the infliction of a fine of 5000 rupees on the Jam or Rajah of Noanuggur, for violating the terms of the covenant into which he had entered; and, moreover, induced the Jam to sign another covenant of even a more stringent character. So signal an example as this—the actual levying of a fine of a large amount on one of the most powerful of the native princes of Guzerat, the recognised head of the Jarejah tribes—could not fail to produce some effect on the community generally. From so prompt and decisive a proof of the resolution of Government to suppress the crime, the brightest results might have been looked for, had only the great principle of supervision been adhered to. But this appears to have been gradually relaxed. The registration of births was neglected, or only performed irregularly; and the withdrawal of this salutary check tempted the Jarejahs to relapse into their former bar-

* The Governorship of St. Helena was originally ceded by Charles II. to the East India Company.

barous custom. Five years only elapsed before Captain Carnac was obliged to report to Government that the philanthropic measures of his predecessor had failed of their hoped-for results; that the violation of the agreement entered into in 1809 by the Jarejahs had become so frequent, that it would be scarcely possible to single out any individual instances for punishment.* It was this discovery which, as we have before noticed, drew from the Bombay Government such unjust imputations and censures on the conduct of Colonel Walker, for failures which were rather to be traced to neglect and apathy in carrying out the preventive measures he had urged on them; and in some degree, perhaps, to the political changes which had, during that period, passed over the country.

Although, however, the crime had again become so general that there was a difficulty in singling out individuals for fine or punishment, it so chanced that there were some few persons who might be advantageously selected for favor. Of these, the most important was the Rajah of Murvee, one of the minor principalities in Guzerat, who had been among the foremost in aiding Colonel Walker in furthering his benevolent plans, and now was found to have given full effect to them in his own family by preserving the lives of two daughters. Captain Carnac, anxious to obtain for this prince a mark of public approval, suggested that the expenses of the marriage of these two daughters should be defrayed out of the public

* In 1817, Captain Ballantine, assistant to Captain Carnac (then in Kattyawar), reported that from December, 1808 (the date of Colonel Walker's report of success), to June, 1817, the number of females preserved had only increased from thirty-two to sixty-three.—Mr. Willoughby's Report.

treasury. This plan, however, was not considered to be advisable, lest it should be regarded as a precedent, and thus lead to the outlay of public money on principles of questionable soundness. Captain Carnac was, however, authorised to confer on the Rajah, in the name of the Court of Directors, a valuable present. All who understand the peculiar constitution of the native mind will at once admit the wisdom of this decision. A costly shawl, a Khillut, or dress of honor, or any such present, would be far more highly esteemed by a native prince than ten times its value in money. It would become an heirloom in his house, and be treasured by his descendants as a lasting mark of the favor of the "Great Sircar"—the East India Company.

Captain Carnac also urged on Government the propriety of establishing a system of spies, and of encouraging informers for the detection of this crime; but these measures were also considered by Government to be inexpedient. Their determination was to "wait upon time."

An opportunity, however, soon offered, which was promptly taken advantage of. Internal feuds in Cutch, and a consequent state of anarchy and danger, called for the interference of the English. In the treaty then entered into* between the two powers, for the restoration of peace and good government, certain clauses were introduced having especial reference to infanticide, by which the Rao himself, and all the Jarejah chiefs, became bound to abolish the practice in their own families, and among their respective clans.

* The treaty bore date October 13, 1819. Wilson's Infanticide.

Still there was no system; not even the most ordinary steps seem to have been taken to enforce the terms of these several agreements. During some seven years, *i.e.* from 1817 to 1824, anything approaching to energetic action in this cause was unknown; all efforts for the suppression of this crime seem to have been suspended. The appointment of Mr. Mountstuart Elphinstone to the Governorship of Bombay did indeed, in some degree, stimulate the zeal which had thus lain dormant. But even this able and enlightened statesman, ever so ready to consult for the amelioration of the native community, seemed to have regarded the difficulties which presented themselves as so formidable, and the prospects of success as so faint and remote, that he was not prepared to renew the struggle with this evil spirit openly and with vigor. "We must be content" (said he, in 1821) "to follow the footsteps of our predecessors (without attempting to go beyond them) in their most meritorious endeavours to discountenance this enormity; and we may safely flatter ourselves that, as the manners of the people become softened by a continuance of tranquillity and good order, they will gradually discontinue a practice which is not more inconsistent with reason than repugnant to natural instinct."

It was, however, during the latter part of Mr. Elphinstone's administration that a very important change was made in the character of the anti-infanticidal measures which his predecessors had adopted. The consideration of the real character and merits of this new principle must be reserved for the next chapter. Here, however, in alluding to it, it may be well to offer a few remarks on the spirit of the former system. This crime had been hitherto generally regarded in Western India as springing from the meanest and most unworthy motives. Such a view being taken of this moral disease, it was natural that the most stringent remedies should be applied. Prohibitory measures were consequently adopted as being the only ones likely to prove effective. The agreements into which the Jarejahs were persuaded to enter contemplated only the suppression of the crime by fear; there was in them nothing that was calculated to remove or eradicate the motives from which it sprang—nothing to wean them voluntarily from so repulsive a custom. If a child was saved, its life would be due to fear of the consequences of a breach of faith rather than to any absence of that earlier fear which originally prompted to the crime.

One word, however, as to the punishments, the fear of which were to operate so effectively. Those Agreements,* noble as were the ends the framers of them had

* The form of agreement, according to which the Rajkoomars pledged themselves to abandon infanticide, was dated Dec. 17, 1789, and ran in the following terms:

"Whereas it hath become known to the Government of the Honorable English East India Company, that we of the tribe of Rajkumars, do not suffer our female children to live, and whereas this is a great crime, as mentioned in the Bretmo Bywunt Pooran (Brahma Vaivartta Purana), where it is said, that killing even a fœtus was as criminal as killing a Brahman; and that for killing a female or woman, the punishment is to suffer in the nerk (Narka) or hell, called Kal Sooter (Kala Sutra), for as many years as there are hairs of that female's body; and that afterwards that person shall be born again, and successively become a leper, and be afflicted with the Zakham; and whereas the British Government in India, whose subjects we are, have an utter detestation of such murderous practices, and we do ourselves acknowledge that, although customary among us, it is highly sinful,—we do, therefore, hereby agree not to commit any longer such detestable acts; and any among us who (which God forbid) shall be hereafter guilty thereof, or shall not bring up and get our daughters married, to the best of our abilities, among those of our caste, shall be expelled from our tribe, and we shall neither eat nor keep society with such person or persons, besides suffering hereafter the punishments in view, were, we venture to think, of an anomalous and questionable character. They present a strange medley of pains and penalties. Based jointly on the authority of the acts of the British Government and the Hindoo Puranas, the violation of them entailed corresponding joint punishments of fine and loss of caste. Now the intrinsic value of the former of these may be easily estimated; from the difficulty of detection, as has been shown, they were perfectly nugatory; the infliction of fines had become "a dead letter." As for the latter, the loss of caste, it is not too much to say that such a threat on our parts was as unbecoming as it was idle; unbecoming it certainly was for a Christian power, by referring to the Puranas and Shastras, and recognising their false

denounced in the above purana and shastra."

The following is a translation of the agreement entered into by the Jarejahs of Kattyawar:

"Whereas the Honorable English Company and Anandrao Gaikawād (Guicowar) Sená Khaskhel Shamsher Bahadur, having set forth to us the dictates of the shastras and the true faith of the Hindoos, as well as that the Brahmá Vaivarttaka Purana declares the killing of children to be a heinous sin—it being written that it is as great an offence to kill an embryo as a Brahman; that to kill one woman is as great a sin as a hundred Brahmans; that to put one child to death is as great a transgression against the divine laws as to kill a hundred women; and that the perpetrators of this sin shall be damned to hell (Kala Sutra), where he shall be infested with as many maggots as he may have hairs on his body, be born again a leper, and debilitated in all his members,—we, Jadeja Dewaji and Kúer Nathu, Zamindars of Gondal (the custom of female infanticide having long prevailed in our caste), do hereby agree for ourselves and for our offspring, as also we bind ourselves in behalf of our relations and their offspring, for ever, for the sake of our own prosperity, and for the credit of the Hindu faith, that we shall from this day renounce this practice; and in default of this, that we acknowledge ourselves offenders against the Sirkars.[1] Moreover, should any one in future commit this offence, we shall expel him from our caste, and he shall be punished according to the pleasure of the two Governments, and the rule of the Shastras."

In both of the foregoing forms of agreement, the translation (and the spelling) given in Dr. Wilson's Infanticide in Western India, p. 41 and pp. 81, 82, have been adopted, as being probably the most correct.

[1] The British and Guicowar Governments.

system of rewards and punishments, to give even the semblance of a sanction to their authority; and no less idle, because to enforce this loss of caste (without the full concurrence of the whole tribe) would be about as practicable in the hands of a Christian Government, however strong, as excommunication from the Church of Christ would have been in those of the "Great Mogul" in the zenith of his power.

CHAPTER III.

EFFORTS IN WESTERN INDIA.

Bombay continued—Under Mr. Elphinstone more persuasive measures introduced—Rewards for preserving daughters—Policy of this questionable—Mr. Willoughby—"Infanticide Fund"—A new era—The whole system resuscitated—The Rao of Rajkote heavily punished—Improvement perceptible, though gradual—Proofs of signal success on Mr. Willoughby's leaving Bombay—Contemporaneous efforts in Cutch, &c.—Mr. Malet, Pottinger, Burnes—Koombees practise it from mercenary motives.

THE new features to which allusion has been made as being introduced at this time, may be thus briefly described; it was the addition of *persuasive* measures to those of a merely *coercive* character, which had hitherto been adopted. The violation of their agreements had, in cases of conviction, been visited with fines; it was now thought that the fines thus inflicted might be thrown into a fund out of which presents of money, &c., might be made towards defraying the marriage expenses entailed on those who, acting up to their agreements, should preserve their daughters. This was no new idea, though now first brought into practice. Mr. J. Duncan, it will be remembered, had entreated permission to adopt such a plan so long before as 1789, with the Rajkoomars at

Benares; Colonel Walker had hinted at it in 1809, while at Baroda, and had again strongly urged it in his Report in 1819; Captain Carnac, his successor, had taken the same view; he had suggested it to Government, not merely in the special case of the Rajah of Murvee, but for general adoption; and Mr. Warden, of the Bombay civil service, had recommended it; yet it was not till 1821 that the plan received official sanction. This delay in adopting it appears to have arisen from a fear, by no means groundless, that the good which was looked for from it was liable to be more than counterbalanced by the evil it might produce. The Jarejahs might, indeed, be persuaded to preserve their children to some extent, when one of the chief motives to their destruction—the enormous outlay required of them in contracting marriages for their daughters—was so much lessened by the promise of public aid. The Rajpoot father, who would defy the watchful eye of the paid spy or the bribed informer to convict him of murder, if an unwelcome daughter should unaccountably disappear at the time of her birth, might yet be tempted to avow that daughter's existence, and to use every means for her preservation, if he felt sure that he should receive some assistance towards her marriage. But, on the other hand, might it not supply a new and powerful motive to other races to resort to the same atrocities for the sake of establishing a claim to similar public aid? Might not the Khutree, or any of the Vaiseea tribes even, be tempted to emulate the daughter-slaying propensities of the Jarejah Rajpoot, that he might qualify himself for becoming a recipient of the public bounty? It was a two-edged sword; it might "cut both ways." It was on this ground that, as has been seen, it was rejected by Government when originally proposed by Mr. Duncan; and on the same ground there had ever since been a reluctance to use it.

Mr. Mountstuart Elphinstone, however, was bold enough to sanction the principle in a modified form, hoping that a prudent and judicious exercise of it might operate beneficially. In a letter to Captain Barnewell (in 1821), who was at that time political agent in Kattyawar, he thus proposed it: "With a view to encourage parents in sparing their female children, you are authorised to throw all the fines levied on chiefs for other offences, as well as for infanticide (after indemnifying the sufferers by each), into a fund to be distributed in proportion to children so preserved."

In this suggestion of Mr. Elphinstone's we see the germ of the "Infanticide Fund," which was afterwards established in Bombay, and which, in a still more modified form and in a subordinate position, formed an important part of the system which was developed by Mr. Willoughby, a Bombay civilian, who has since risen to take his place in the East India "Direction," as one of the first of the Directors nominated by Government. Although we are unable to follow out in detail the workings and the results of that system, which has gained for Mr. Willoughby a position second to none in the list of those who have stood forth as the champions of humanity in India, and which has placed his name beside those of Duncan and Walker, where he reflects as much honor as he receives from the connexion, we feel assured that in every stage of his distinguished Indian career, whether as assistant at the Baroda Residency, or as Resident at that Court, in the Secretariat, or at the Council Board, he has left behind not only signs of great intellectual power, but also of high philanthropic zeal in an unceasing endeavour to rescue these helpless victims of Rajpoot pride and poverty from an untimely end. To him, by universal consent, Bombay is indebted for a revival of that energetic action which had marked the days of Duncan and Walker, and which, but for an occasional, irregular, transient sign of life, might, during the intervening years of apathy, have been regarded as extinct. With his name is especially connected the Bombay "Infanticide Fund," the principles of which cannot be better explained than in his own words. "The Infanticide Fund was established in 1825. It is composed of all fines under 20,000 rupees imposed upon tributaries for breaches of the peace, or other misconduct, and of realisation under the head of Mohsullee. The British Government set the example; his Highness the Guicowar being subsequently induced to consent that all fines imposed upon his tributaries should be similarly appropriated. From this source occasional remission of tribute, presents to chiefs, and pecuniary assistance on the marriage of their daughters, have been granted to those who have practically renounced the custom; and another mode of testifying approbation to those who have preserved their daughters is by postponing the payment of the tribute to suit their convenience."* It will be seen at once how vast an improve-

* Mr. Willoughby's Report.

ment this was on all preceding systems. It supplied new and powerful motives to the Jarejahs for the preservation of their daughters, without overlooking the necessity of retaining such a system of *surveillance* as might prevent their destruction. This great scheme, which he may be said to have originated, was composed of the following parts: Firstly, a census of the Jarejah tribes was to be at once prepared, showing the disparity of the sexes as then existing. Secondly, a regular half-yearly return of births, betrothals, marriages, and deaths was required from each Jarejah chief for his own clan. Thirdly, the political agent was called on to send in to Government an annual report on the subject of infanticide, based on those half-yearly returns, and such other information as he might obtain. Fourthly, a proclamation was to be issued throughout the Jarejah tribes, assuring them of the full determination of Government to mark with its approval or displeasure, to reward or punish, every individual as he might observe or violate the terms of the agreement. Fifthly, every Rajpoot was enjoined to stipulate at every marriage contract of a daughter with a Jarejah that any female offspring from such union should be preserved; and, Sixthly, sums of money, or presents of clothes or ornaments, were to be given out of the "Infanticide Fund" to such Jarejahs as had adhered to their engagements and preserved their daughters. Such was the general scope of the measures recommended and introduced by Mr. Willoughby, as set forth at length in his able Report of 1834—"measures" of which it has been well said that, "though exhibiting nothing essentially new or untried, they yet presented in improved and more comprehensive forms the matured suggestions of his predecessors."*

The Bombay Government were soon called on to show how far they were prepared to give full effect to the system now introduced. A most flagrant violation of the agreement on the part of the Thakoor, or chief of Rajkote, a small principality in Guzerat, was reported by Mr. Willoughby, and at his suggestion a heavy fine, no less a sum than *twelve thousand rupees*, was inflicted on the Thakoor, and, to ensure payment, his estate was placed under attachment until the fine should be paid. A short time after, another petty chief, under circumstances of peculiar atrocity, was sentenced to twelve months' imprisonment and a fine of three thousand rupees, or in default of payment, a further imprisonment of two years. These examples, with others of less note and on a smaller scale, sufficed to prove to the Jarejahs that the agreements into which they had entered were *realities*, and that the British Government would not suffer them to be violated with impunity.

Nevertheless, the reports which were sent in from time to time by Mr. Willoughby's successors at Baroda, Mr. Erskine, Captain Jacob, and Captain Lang, while they, in some instances, betray a want of consistency with each other, showing how almost impossible it was to obtain accurate information respecting the birth of children under such circumstances, disclose the fact that infanticide was not yet being so effectually suppressed as

* Calcutta Review, No. II. p. 423, from which source the greater part of the information respecting this period has been obtained, in the absence of original and authentic documents.

might have been reasonably expected under such a vigorous and stringent *régime.* Captain Jacob, in 1841, was obliged to qualify his report of the successful working of these measures in some districts by the disheartening announcement that in others there was little, if any, sign of improvement. In one district he found, in a population of 122, *only seven females;* in another, during four years "not a single female had escaped the ruthless effects of Jarejah pride." Still, on the whole, the new system was believed to be making itself generally felt. Although in some villages, or among some families, the crime appeared to have received no check, yet in the returns for the whole country there was a decided improvement. The disparity of the sexes was beginning to diminish. Captain Jacob felt justified in expressing himself thus favorably of the general results up to that time: "It must be highly gratifying," he said, "to those benevolent men who had labored for the suppression of infanticide, to see the progressive return to the order of nature in the relative proportion of the sexes, that must be attributed to their labor alone." And the Bombay Government acknowledged thus warmly the encouraging nature of the Reports: "The complete suppression of the crime, originating in ignorance, prejudice, and false pride, must doubtless be the work of time, yet, looking back to the past, and seeing how much had been accomplished within the last few years, they were encouraged strongly to hope that a steady, constant perseverance in the measures in operation would in the end be rewarded by full and complete success."

Eight years afterwards, in 1849, Major Lang, who had in the mean time succeeded to the political agency at Kattyawar, communicated still more gladdening intelligence of the progress of the anti-infanticidal movement. "The proportion of female children to males in all the tribes is now so nearly equal, and the progressive increase of the female population so regular, that, if the returns can be depended upon in other respects, there would be every ground for believing that the practice of infanticide must have become almost entirely extinct in this province."

This steady, gradual approximation of the sexes cannot be better shown than by inserting a short tabular statement of the Jarejah population during the five years from 1845 to 1850, inclusive:*

	1845.	1846.	1847.	1848.	1849.	1850.
Males	6617	6600	6844	7356	7353	7502
Females	2334	2429	2779	3090	3273	3423

From which it appears that, whereas in 1817 the number of females known to have been preserved, according to Mr. Willoughby's Report, had only been 63, within thirty years the proportion of females to males had risen to nearly one-third, and in six years more this disparity had been still more reduced, and the number of females amounted to nearly one-half that of the males.

The proportionate increase of the female population is

* This table is taken from Kaye's Administration of the East India Company.

also shown more clearly by the registered births of the years 1850 and 1851. In the former there were 267 female infants born to 292 males, and in the latter 216 of the one to 222 of the other; thus the number of boys over girls in 1850 was 25, and in the following year *only six*.

Mr. Willoughby, the originator of these later measures, did not retire from India until 1851—till he had been permitted to witness the full realisation of his philanthropic hopes, and therein to reap the reward of his labors. He admitted that the success had been far greater and much more rapid than the most sanguine, acquainted with the real difficulties of the case, could have anticipated. "I recollect," he said, when about to leave Bombay, "that by some whose opinions I valued, I was thought to have invaded too strictly the sanctity of Rajpoot domestic privacy, and that the measures I had recourse to were too harsh, and likely to outrage the feelings of the whole Rajpoot community. But I argued that those philanthropic men, Governor Duncan and Colonel Walker, never intended that the engagements which they induced the Jarejahs to enter into should be waste paper; and although I was aware that I was touching on delicate ground, I felt assured that I should find a powerful ally in those feelings of parental affection which exist in the human breast in every stage and degree of civilisation. The result has certainly proved that I was not mistaken."

It will be observed that the foregoing account has, with one or two slight exceptions, been confined to the history of the anti-infanticidal measures which were adopted in Kattyawar or Guzerat, and little or no mention is made of what was being done in the adjacent peninsula of Cutch, where also a large body of Jarejah Rajpoots are found. This arrangement was adopted for the following reasons: The Baroda Residency supplied the most energetic opponents of this "child murder;" there the movement may be said to have originated; from thence the most important measures for its suppression emanated; and those adopted in Cutch were, generally speaking, of the same character, indeed, a part of the same system; and by tracing out the working of that system in the one branch, it was hoped that the successive measures and changes introduced might be better explained, and the thread of the narrative preserved unbroken.

Not that those who stood forward as the champions of humanity in Cutch should be passed over in silence. Here were laboring, among others, Mr. Malet,* of the Bombay civil service, Captain Melvill, Mr. Lumsden, &c.; nor may we omit the names of two officers, whose diplomatic careers commenced among the Jarejah Rajpoots of Cutch, but whose after-deeds obtained for them a prominent place in the annals of their country—Major (afterwards Sir Henry) Pottinger, the future dictator of terms to the refractory Chinese, and the Governor of two British colonies, the Cape and Madras; and also Captain (better known by his later title, Sir Alexander) Burnes, the victim of Affghan treachery and mismanagement.

To prove that the labors of these men were not with-

* Mr. Malet was afterwards removed to the political agency at Kattyawar.

out effect, even if less successful than the movement had been in Guzerat during the same period, it will be enough to quote from the statistical returns the numbers of males and females of all ages among the Jarejahs of Cutch, as given for the undermentioned years. There were—

	IN 1842.	IN 1847.	IN 1852.
Males	6208	6445	6761
Females	701	1130	1723

Thus showing that in ten years the number of females had been considerably more than doubled, while that of the males had not increased one-tenth. This was unimpeachable testimony to the success of the measures for the suppression of female infanticide.

A few words may be added in this place with reference to another class of Hindoos, who, though not connected with the great Rajpoot family, are still proved to be very much addicted to this crime. In the tract of land lying between Guzerat and the Gulf of Cambay on the one side, and the Rajpootana States on the other, over the whole range of country from Ahmedabad on the north to Baroche on the south, are found a tribe called Koombees, no longer of the Kshutreea, or military order, like their neighbour Rajpoots, but belonging to the Khutree caste.* Among this people the practice of female infanticide seems to be very prevalent. Lying

* On the supposed difference between Kshutreeas and Khutrees, see *infra*, chap. vii. p. 112.

on both sides of the Myhee, this river seems to form a social, no less than a geographical, separation between the two classes. Those on the north side claim a superiority over their more southern kinsmen, and only consent to allow their sons to marry the daughters of the lower grades on condition of receiving a large sum of money in return for what they consider their condescension and sacrifice of dignity; and to make the most of this claim, and to turn it to account in a pecuniary way, the higher class *destroy their own daughters*, that their young men may be driven to the south for their wives and the accompanying *douceur*. To such an extent has this principle been established, that the payment of dowry with their daughters on the part of the more southern Koombees has become a regular and recognised source of revenue to their more fortunate brethren of the north.

Whether any and what measures have been adopted to put an end to this speculating child-murder we have no means of learning.

In concluding this chapter, the author can only express his regret, if the account of this most interesting period in the history of the anti-infanticidal movement in Bombay should seem to be meagre and incomplete. The work itself aspired to be nothing more than a sketch of the course pursued by a Christian people for the suppression of a most inhuman practice among their heathen dependents. With this view the work was undertaken; and although any materials from which this part of the history might have been filled in, had they been available at the time, would have been most gladly taken advantage of, yet, from the want of such, and from the knowledge that this particular period was being treated of by one of the most eminent Bombay missionaries, the writer was well content to leave it to his far more able pen. After the foregoing chapter was completed, the looked-for work, "Dr. Wilson's Infanticide in Western India," appeared in print. It would then have been easy out of that mine of information to work up an account of this period more perfectly; but the doing so would also have involved a departure from the original plan. The author has, therefore, contented himself with introducing here and there from that work a few remarks corroborative of the statements previously made, and inserting one or two extracts which tended to carry on his narrative to a later period. For these he begs to offer his grateful acknowledgments, and ventures to advise the reader who may wish for a deeper insight into these measures, to consult that book itself, in which an almost lifelong local experience, and access to the most authentic information, have enabled Dr. Wilson to do full justice to the subject.

CHAPTER IV.

RAJPOOTANA AND MALWA.

Prevalence of the crime discovered by Mr. L. Wilkinson—Sumptuary measures recommended—Jyepore, Joudpore, Ajmeer, &c.—Colonel Sutherland, Captains Thoresby and Ludlow—The extortion of Bhâts and Chârans restrained by reducing scale of marriage expenses—Mairwarrah—Colonel Hall—Convenes Punchayut—Persuades Mairs to reduce marriage expenses—Success complete—Dr. Wilson's Infanticide in Western India.

PASSING eastward from the land of the Jarejah and the Koombee, we enter on the classic ground of Rajpoot history, the country called, after themselves, "Rajpootana," or "Rajasthan," and southward, between that and the Nerbudda river, lies the separate principality of Malwa. Here is, in reality, the Rajpoot stronghold. In Malwa and the several Rajpootana states is to be found some of the purest and proudest blood of that once royal race.* The states of Odeypore, Jyepore, Ajmeer, Joudpore, &c., vie with each other in claiming superiority of descent; and in so genial a soil it is but natural that this pride of birth should be found to bear its bitter fruit of infanticide. First among the philanthropists whose names are connected with these Rajpoot Courts, was

* For a full account of the Rajpoot history, see Tod's Rajasthan.

Mr. Launcelot Wilkinson, of the Bombay civil service. Although Malwa was more particularly the field of his labors, it was in the northern states of Odeypore and Jyepore that he first discovered the existence of this crime. In 1821, Sir John Malcolm had officially reported to Government to the following effect: "Infanticide," he said, "in Malwa is not known among the lower classes; this shocking usage still remains among some Rajpoot chiefs of high rank and small fortunes, who, from a despair of obtaining a suitable marriage for their daughters, are led by an infatuated pride to become the destroyers of their own offspring. The usage is, however, on the decline, and every effort has been made to prevent the frequent recurrence of this crime." Yet, fifteen years after, Mr. L. Wilkinson communicated to Government that "an intelligent Rajpoot chief" had stated it as his opinion "that not less than twenty thousand infants were annually destroyed in Malwa and Rajpootana;" and as he himself travelled over this country, in the capacity of political agent, he found everywhere too confirmatory proofs of the prevalence of the crime to leave any room for hope that the statement of the Rajpoot chief was even an exaggeration. It would be impossible to follow Mr. Wilkinson step by step through the investigations he instituted, and the melancholy discoveries he made; it will suffice to sum up all in his own words, that the result of his inquiries "must fully satisfy every one that female infanticide is carried on to a frightful extent throughout Malwa and Rajpootana."

The information thus gathered from all quarters by means of personal inquiry during his tour through the several states, led Mr. Wilkinson to look with little favor on the coercive system which had been adopted in Kattyawar; he was induced to put more faith in the efficacy of measures of a sumptuary nature, and to a general elevation of the moral character by education. He declared his conviction that "formal renunciations of the practice by the rajahs and chiefs were not likely to prove by any means efficient for the extinction of the practice;" and that "penal enactments not supported by public opinion were a dead letter." To Mr. Wilkinson, therefore, is the anti-infanticidal movement indebted for the first suggestion that sumptuary measures should be introduced in combination with those of a coercive character.

It has been remarked that the rival Rajpoot chiefs of the more important states, such as Odeypore, Jyepore, and Ajmeer, vied with each other in claiming superiority of birth and rank. From the existence of this feeling a new difficulty arose, which was scarcely known among the Jarejahs, who were all of one race, and among whom the relative degrees of rank were consequently more defined and recognised. So great, however, was the jealousy of these rival Rajpoot chiefs, and their reluctance to intermarry, that it became necessary to remove, if possible, this feeling at the outset, in order to ensure the co-operation and the example of the chiefs themselves, for the sake of giving full effect to the measures among their respective clansmen. With this view, Mr. Wilkinson urged them, and successfully, to enter into an agreement among themselves to the effect that no Rajpoot should give a daughter in marriage into, or receive one from, any clan or house which would not pledge itself to reciprocate such alliance when required.*

The opinion formed by Mr. Wilkinson in favor of a system of sumptuary arrangements appears to have been fully concurred in by the several officers who subsequently held official connexion with the Rajpoot States. Of these, the more active were Colonel Sutherland, Captain Thoresby, and Captain Ludlow.

It would appear that these Rajpoots candidly avowed not only the perpetration of the crime, but also the exorbitant marriage expenditure as the chief motive that prompted them to it. Whatever weight pride of birth originally may have had, or still retained among them, they did not hesitate to account for their unnatural conduct on the other principle. "Pay our daughters' marriage portions and they shall live," was, according to Bishop

* Of the extent to which this pride of birth and mutual rivalry was really carried, the following extract from Kaye's "Life and Correspondence of Lord Metcalfe" will afford a striking illustration. Sir C. Metcalfe (in 1814), while Resident at Delhi, was instructed to inquire into the matrimonial connexions which were formed between the Mogul princes and the daughters of the Rajpoot Rajahs. On the information of the Joudpore Vakeel, whom he describes as a "most respectable and well-informed old man," Sir Charles thus writes on the subject: "It was first proposed to the Rajpoot Rajahs to form a connexion with the imperial family by taking in marriage imperial princesses; but this proposal was rejected, as such a communication would have polluted the blood of the Rajahs' families, and would have been utter abomination for ever; they were glad to effect their escape from so alarming a danger by sacrificing their own daughters, who were considered as dead from the time of their connexion with the emperors. After the ice had been once broken by the formation of a connexion of this kind, it came to be considered a custom, and ceased to be objectionable. A connexion with the emperors was thought desirable for political purposes; and the rivalship of the Rajahs of Jyepore and Joudpore made both occasionally press forward with their daughters, each being jealous when such a connexion was formed by the other. Nevertheless, the daughters were considered dead and gone, though their posthumous influence was an object of desire to their fathers."—(Vol. i. pp. 416, 417.) Thus policy triumphed over pride, and saved the lives of a few Rajpootana princesses, who must otherwise have been sacrificed in infancy; for there was little hope that the rival houses of Jyepore and Joudpore would yield to each other that admission of equality

Heber,* the reply of Rajpoots to British officers when remonstrated with. Now the men in whom the political management of these states was at that time vested were not disposed to adopt the plan suggested, nor to admit the principle even to the extent to which it had been sanctioned in the formation of the Bombay Infanticide Fund; at the same time, the confession of the Rajpoots gave them a clue to the root of the evil of which they were not slow to avail themselves. They at once traced this system of extravagant marriage expenditure to the interested influence of the Bhâts and Chârans† (of whom mention has been already made in the first chapter); and that influence they set themselves steadfastly to counteract.

It was once suggested to the Bombay Government, we think by Major Jacob, that as this class of men were the chief cause of such enormous sums being expended at marriages, some restriction should be put on the demands of this rapacious fraternity. To this the Government objected, lest such restriction from excess should imply a recognition and sanction of the principle itself. The Rajpootana officials resolved on trying another plan for overthrowing this system of mendicancy. Without any allusion to the extortion of these harpies, they induced the Rajpoots to enter into an agreement among themselves to reduce the whole rate of marriage expenditure, so that in no case should it exceed one-tenth of the annual income

or superiority involved in a matrimonial alliance, which they so reluctantly, and only from state expediency, conceded to the Delhi princes.

* Heber's Journal, chap. xxiv.

† Captain Ludlow reported that sometimes three-fourths of a year's income would be exacted at a single marriage by the Bhâts and Chârans.

of the bride's father. On this reduced sum there were so many claimants in the bridegroom's family that but little was left for Bhâts and Chârans. The domestic or village bard might still receive some trifle as a "guerdon,"

> "To praise the hand that paid his pains,"

but there was no longer any spoil worth the gathering to lure the troops of "foreign" vagabonds.

This plan was first put in force by Captain Ludlow, in Jyepore; and the example of that state was gladly followed by the others. They were all eager to emancipate themselves from the tyranny, and to be free of the tax of which they had so long been the victims. And thus the influence of men who had been the terror of Rajpootana was thoroughly broken down.*

In the heart of Rajpootana, surrounded by the races of high-caste Hindoos, of whom we have been speaking, is a race called Mairs, an abbreviation of the name of the district they inhabit—Mairwarrah, or "the region of hills"—who are proved to resemble the Rajpoots, among whom they live, in their infanticidal habits. An account of this people should more properly be introduced in a subsequent chapter; but their geographical position, and, moreover, the measures adopted among them for the suppression of this crime, seem to connect them so closely with this part of our narrative, that they may not inaptly find a place here. According to Colonel Tod, the historian of Rajasthan, the Mairs are a branch of the Ménas, one

* Kaye's Administration of the East India Company, p. 576.

of the aboriginal tribes of India. The successive conquests of the Hindoos and the Mahomedans have driven them from their native plains to seek for shelter among the mountain fastnesses, where they have succeeded in escaping the yoke of those earlier conquerors, and in defying the more recent attacks of the neighbouring Mahrattas. The perpetration of the crime of infanticide was first discovered to exist among them in 1827, by Captain Hall, whose official position in that district gave him the opportunity of detecting it, and an influence which he most prudently exercised for its suppression. Among these Mairs, as among their neighbour Rajpoots, the expenditure of enormous sums on the marriage of their daughters may be regarded as the most powerful motive to this inhuman custom. Yet there was a remarkable difference between the two systems. Among the Rajpoots the main expenditure lay on the father of the bride; whereas among the Mairs it was on the side of the bridegroom's family. This expenditure was regulated by a universally received scale of payments, which, however exorbitant, was retained as sacred and unalterable. The Rajpoot, as we have seen, had to pay for a husband for his daughter; the Mairwarrah father had to buy a wife for his son. The one, then, lest he should be unable to marry and portion his daughter worthily; the other, lest his should be left unmarried because no one was prepared to pay the high price set on her—both murdered them in infancy to avoid the risk of disgrace. In Mairwarrah, Colonel Hall labored for many years to check this practice. He tried a simple plan, adapted to a simple-minded race. He pointed out the folly of regarding as sacred and inviolable those exorbitant marriage payments under which they were groaning. Those rates had been voluntarily adopted at first, and might at any time be reduced. By such arguments he induced them to convene a general Punchayut,* or meeting of their "Council," and to draw up a greatly-modified scale of marriage payments. They did so; and (to use the words of one who twenty years after succeeded Colonel Hall,† and witnessed the result of his system) "thus Infanticide received its death-blow in Mairwarrah."

* This word literally means five, that being the number of members of which their councils generally consist, or which constitutes a "quorum."

† Colonel Dixon's Mairwarrah.

CHAPTER V.

EFFORTS IN AZIMGHUR.

Bengal—Little attempt made towards suppressing the crime after Duncan's removal to Bombay, in consequence of ceaseless wars—Again brought to notice by Mr. Thomason at Azimghur—Mr. R. Montgomery, then his assistant, afterwards magistrate of Allahabad, discovered the crime to be practised by Rajpoots on the Rewah frontier—Adopted and very judiciously applied a system of supervision with great success—Obtained a reward for a Rajpoot who had greatly aided him—Effects of Mr. Montgomery's labours still visible in the Allahabad district.

WITH Mr. Duncan, who discovered the existence of female infanticide among the Rajkoomar Rajpoots, near Benares, we have passed over to the Western Presidency, to trace the successive measures which during fifty years were taken to suppress this crime among the Rajpoots of Kattyawar and Cutch, and those of Malwa and Rajpootana. We must now return to Bengal, and examine what progress the movement, which really had its origin in this Presidency, made during the period which has elapsed since the transfer of Mr. Duncan's philanthropic labors to Bombay. For nearly forty years the subject of Infanticide seems to have had comparatively no place in the councils of the Bengal Presidency, or the offices of the local magistracy. The only public allusion to it that we have been able to discover was the issue, in 1804, of a proclamation prohibiting it, which was afterwards notified under the orders of the Bareilly Court of Circuit, dated 30th September, 1809.

Yet, in drawing any comparison between the efforts which during that interval were being made in Bombay, and the seeming inactivity which prevailed in Bengal, it should be borne in mind that it was a period in which the former Presidency lay well-nigh becalmed in a sea of peace, which only the lessening billows of some distant convulsion occasionally ruffled, while the other was the centre of every such political convulsion—the Maëlstrom of warfare and intrigue. It were enough to mention that between the days of good Jonathan Duncan at Benares and the period at which the subject of infanticide was renewed in Bengal, the names of Wellesley, Lake, and Ochterlony had become part of Indian history; that Scindiah and Holkar had disappeared from the political stage of Central and North-Western India; that the Mahratta and the Pindarree had sunk beneath the weight of that power which they had drawn down upon themselves; that from Benares—in Duncan's day a recently-acquired possession—English arms had been carried successfully to the banks of the Sutlej; that the throne of Akbar and the musnud of the Mogul had been involuntarily, yet irresistibly, absorbed into the vortex of English rule; and the name of England had found its way to the Holy City of Umritsur, and made her influence to be felt at the gates of Lahore! When it is remembered that during those forty years of progress new conquests had to be consolidated, new countries peaceably settled, and new subjects conciliated, it will be the less wondered at that Bengal was behind the sister Presidency in suffering even so inhuman a crime as this female infanticide, so secretly and subtilely perpetrated, to escape notice.

The revival of the subject, however, after so long an interval, is connected with the name of one to whose memory, revered as it so justly is by all classes for his many acts of public benefit and of true Christian philanthropy, the humble chronicler of the anti-infanticidal movement may be permitted to offer a passing tribute of respect. The ready encouragement and co-operation which Mr. Thomason gave, as Lieutenant-Governor of the North-West Provinces, to every effort for the suppression of this crime, is proclaimed in various official documents; but we believe it is not so generally known that he it was to whom Bengal is really, though indirectly, indebted for again bringing the subject forward. In the year 1836, Mr. Thomason, while magistrate and collector of Azimghur, first had his attention directed to the prevalence of this custom, and his zeal kindled for its suppression. He found it to be practised by the Rajpoots of the Baees, Rughunsee, and Gowtum tribes, who resided chiefly on the borders of the Oude territory. Among a body of Rajpoots, numbering some ten thousand, "not a single daughter was forthcoming." The manner in which the fact was brought to his notice is so interestingly described by him, that we give it in his own words: "I do not think it is generally known that the horrible practice so extensively prevails even at our own doors. I myself discovered it accidentally whilst engaged in revising the settlement of the Pergunnah, and encamped in that very 'Tuppah'* (of Kooha). In conversation with some of the Zemindars, I happened to mention one of them as the son-in-law† of another. The mistake raised a sarcastic laugh, which was explained by the brief exclamation of a bystander: 'Where will you find a daughter in Kooha?' Inquiry once roused, the truth was palpable. They freely admitted the practice themselves; and it was a matter of notoriety."‡

These Baees Rajpoots of Kooha, Mr. Thomason says, "are a fine, manly, independent race of men. There are few whom I have seen of more prepossessing address. Their tribe have formed of old high alliances, and they have served on regal establishments. . . . . . . They, of course, pride themselves on giving their daughters in marriage only to the members of certain tribes on an equality with themselves, or their superiors. Matches are difficult to be obtained, and attended with great expense, which they can ill bear, and are almost certain to cause the alienation of the whole, or a great part, of their hereditary lands. Hence the birth of a daughter is considered a most serious calamity, and the unfortunate infant is very seldom spared."

In dealing with such a crime, he justly observed, that "as it arises out of their social state, a police is powerless for its correction. So long as the society in which the perpetrators of the crime move can tolerate and pal-

* Tuppah, sub-division of a district.

† We have already remarked that the relationship of a father-in-law implies inferiority, and is often a term of scorn.

‡ Extracted from a letter of Mr. Thomason's to the Agra Government, dated Feb. 12, 1836.

liate such enormities, the civil power must fail to prevent or correct them."

His hope was to check it rather by the exercise of personal influence and reasoning than by any system of coercion; and he was most fortunate in possessing as his Tehseeldar, or chief native revenue officer of that district, a man who was eager to co-operate with him and to further his humane efforts; and by his aid the crime appears to have been partially arrested. So highly did Mr. Thomason appreciate the services of this man, that on his recommendation Government presented him with a Khillut, or dress of honor, to mark their approval of his conduct.

Mr. R. Montgomery, of whom much mention will be made hereafter, was at that time assistant to Mr. Thomason, and was thus first brought into contact with this inhuman practice, and first imbibed that zeal for its abolition which has subsequently marked his judicial career. In 1839 he was appointed to the magistracy of Allahabad; and when entering upon an examination of his new district, his attention was naturally directed to this point. The existence of the practice in the Pergunnah Barra, lying on the borders of the Rewah territory, was soon brought to light, as prevailing to a frightful extent among three Rajpoot tribes: Purharrs, Cutchwas, and Bedourias. He proceeded at once to the Pergunnah, and assembled the heads of the different families, hoping that by persuasion and exhortation he might induce them to relinquish the practice; but finding this of no avail, he determined to try more vigorous measures.

"In the first place," he says, "I appointed a Chupprasee* to reside in each village, whose sole duty it was to report the birth of a female child in the families of any of the above classes of Rajpoots; I also bound the Goorait,† Chowkedar, and midwives, under a heavy penalty, to report separately each birth at the Thannah, the four thus acting as a check on each other; I directed the Thannadar, on the death of any female infant being reported, to hold an inquest on the body, and afterwards to transmit it to the civil surgeon for examination. I associated the Tehseeldar with the Thannadar, in order to ensure a more efficient superintendence; and promised them both handsome rewards, if I should be hereafter satisfied that they, by their joint efforts, had put a stop to the horrible practice.

"I am happy to state that, as far as I am able to judge, the method I have pursued has been attended with perfect success. It is only two months since the plan came into operation, and of four female infants that have since been born, three are alive.‡

* A Chupprassee literally means a man wearing a badge; the common name of a messenger.

† An inferior village constable or runner. Chowkedar, a watchman.

‡ One died; and as this one was killed in the usual way, by administering the juice of the mudar plant, Mr. Montgomery details the particulars, in order to show that his arrangements, so far as he could judge, had been successful in bringing the murder to light:

"The infant was born on the 10th of December, a report of which was immediately made to the Thannah. The Jemadar was deputed to see the child, and on his way met the midwife, who was also coming to report; she returned with the Jemadar's party, and, on lifting up the cloth under which the infant was lying, they found it dying; the midwife declared that a few hours before she had left it strong and well, and that it must have been poisoned. The parents affirmed that its death was caused by lockjaw; they were immediately taken up and conveyed to the Thannah, together with a slave girl who lived in the house, and the body was sent to the surgeon for examination. The slave girl at first denied all knowledge of the affair, but at last confessed that the infant's

". . . . . . As I learned that the practice prevails in the Rewah territory, and that some families have left Barra in order to escape our police, I addressed a communication to the Rajah on the subject, and he has promised to do all in his power to put down the practice. I would suggest the Government should also bring the subject to the notice of the Rajah."*

The state of Rewah, here referred to, is a small independent principality on the Bundelcund side of the Allahabad district. It was then reported, and is still believed to be, one of the greatest obstacles to the effectual working out of any system of compulsion or espionage for the suppression of this practice; being one of those "sanctuaries" for the crime (to which allusion has been already made) into which the Rajpoot's wife retires when far advanced in pregnancy, and returns with or without a child, as she has been delivered of a boy or a girl.

A year later Mr. Montgomery says, "I am happy to be able to report that the crime of infanticide is fast decreasing in Barra. There are now fourteen female children alive, whilst last year I only reported three.

". . . . . The greatest vigilance is still requisite, and on my twice visiting the Pergunnah this year, I was

grandmother had brought some of the mudar juice, and administered it to the infant on the departure of the midwife to the Thannah; she also stated that the mother of the child at first refused to allow the mudar juice to be given, but at the entreaty of her husband at last consented. The surgeon deposed that he found the juice of the mudar plant in the child's stomach, which caused its death; the case is now pending before the session judge, and I trust the parties will be convicted. It will do more towards stopping the practice than anything else; and the fact of the parties being taken up has already caused a great sensation in the Pergunnah."

* Extracted from the Annual Police Report of Zillah Allahabad for the year 1840, dated Jan. 28, 1841.

most particular in looking into and inquiring after the arrangements I had made for putting it down."*

Again, in November, 1842, Mr. Montgomery reported further progress; that, although the crime appeared to be far more prevalent than he at first imagined, the number of girls then preserved amounted to twenty-eight; and he expressed his belief that, "now that so many girls are alive, the minds of the people are beginning to get reconciled to the custom of sparing them:" and he entertained great hopes that there would for the future, with ordinary care, be little difficulty in suppressing it altogether.†

In Azimghur Mr. Montgomery had been one of those deputed to present the Khillut to the Tehseeldar; and we now find him delighting to bring to the notice of Government one Taboo Singh, a Chundele Rajpoot, an inhabitant of the Pergunnah of Burra, to whom he was indebted for the first information regarding the practice of infanticide, and through whose exertions he had been able to make so much progress towards stopping it. "Taboo Singh," he said, "is a poor man, and has followed out his plans with a degree of perseverance and energy quite uncommon to a native, and apparently without looking for any return. His life has been in danger several times from the inhabitants of the different villages, who threatened him with death if ever the opportunity is afforded them." Being a very poor man, a similar present to that received by the Tehseeldar of

* Extracted from the Annual Police Report for 1841.

† Letter to R. Lowther, Esq., Commissioner of the Allahabad Division, dated Nov. 10, 1842.

Azimghur would have been comparatively valueless to him; therefore, at the suggestion of Mr. Montgomery, Government presented Taboo Singh with 500 rupees—a far more substantial and acceptable recognition of his services.

To Mr. Montgomery, then, is due the honor of having again brought the subject of infanticide to public notice, after the long oblivion into which it had been suffered to fall; and of instituting measures which (to use the words of the able author of "Notes on the North-Western Provinces") "bear the practical stamp which has marked all the proceedings of that distinguished public officer." In them we see the fruits of that insight into the existence of the crime which his original association with Mr. Thomason had imparted to him, and of that zeal for its suppression which, when once aroused, has never been allowed to slumber. The subsequent history of those measures we have not the means of following up; but that they have not been without lasting effect, we gladly avail ourselves of permission to adduce the testimony of the present magistrate of Allahabad,* who says, "When Mr. Montgomery undertook the measures, female children were unknown; and there are now close upon a hundred, from fourteen years downwards."

* M. H. Court, Esq., B.C.S.

CHAPTER VI.

EFFORTS IN MYNPOOREE.

The famine of 1838—Its horrors—Its effects for good—Formation of orphan school at Secundra, and Great Ganges Canal—Led to discovery of female infanticide among Chohan Rajpoots of Mynpooree—Mr. H. Unwin, the magistrate, adopts a system of inspection—Granddaughter born to the old Rajah of Mynpooree—Success of measures—System extended to neighbouring districts—Mr. Charles Raikes succeeds Mr. Unwin—Attacks marriage expenses—Holds a meeting at Sumaou—Persuades the Rajpoots by self-legislation to reduce rates of marriage expenses—Undertakes to secure them from Bhâts and beggars—Holds a larger gathering—The Mynpooree meeting for all neighbouring Rajpoots—The reduced scales eagerly adopted—Grateful acknowledgments of Gujadhur Singh—At Mr. Thomason's solicitation prepares the "Letter to the Rajpoots"—Is appointed Commissioner of Lahore.

THE year 1838 is memorable in the annals of India for the ravages of a famine of unprecedented severity in the Upper Provinces. In a country where, notwithstanding the partial prevalence of irrigation from wells, so much depends upon the weather, where "the former and the latter rain in their season" are the main source of vegetation, a drought is a calamity which cannot be averted or provided against. When it comes, it brings in its train famine and death. Such was the dreadful visitation of 1838. Natives died of starvation at the rate of ten thousand a month. The very rivers were choked up with the bodies of the dead. Mothers were known to consign their children alive into a watery grave, that they might be spared the agony of witnessing the death-struggles from hunger which they could not alleviate. Others were eager to sell them for food to satisfy their own cravings. In short, the horrors of that famine, save only that it lacked the further miseries of war, bore no faint resemblance to those of that judicial visitation which devastated the "hemmed and famishing Jerusalem."

During such a season all ordinary public duties were of necessity in abeyance. Kutcherees* were closed for want of suitors. Men were more eager for food than for justice. The magistrate suspended, for the time, his judicial and fiscal functions, to become the almoner of public bounty among the tens of thousands that were perishing around him.

Then was verified that Eastern proverb, "Adversity is like the period of the former and latter rain—cold, comfortless, unfriendly to man and beast; yet from these come the flower and the fruit, the date, the rose, and pomegranate."† That famine was the seed-time of a Christian mission. Three hundred and fifty children, whom that famine had orphaned, found a home at Secundra; that tomb erected by the great Akbar over his Christian wife was converted into an asylum for their reception; and there those "brands plucked from the burning" formed the nucleus of a Christian colony amid the ruins of Moslem pride.‡

* Kutcherees are courts of justice, offices for transacting all public business.

† The reader scarcely needs to be reminded that he is indebted to Sir Walter Scott for this beautiful proverb. It occurs in the "Talisman."

‡ Such is the origin of the orphan

To this famine, too, may be traced the construction of that masterpiece of engineering talent with which the names of Thomason and Cautley are so eminently connected—the Great Ganges Canal; a work which, in grandeur of design and wisdom of purpose, throws into the shade all, even the greatest, works of the Mahomedan emperors; one which, humanly speaking, has rendered impossible the recurrence of such a famine in that district; for though the heavens may be for a time shut up, and the clouds withhold their rain, yet so long as the "eternal snows" rest on the Himalayan heights, and the Indian sun retains his power, the stream of the Ganges can never fail; its snow-melted waters will still flow on, and, brought down through this broad channel, will be dispersed over the length and breadth of the parched Doab,* and even in time of drought "the land will give her increase."

But there were other beneficial measures, though not of such vastness or importance, of more immediate effect, to which this sore visitation gave rise. It brought the magistrate into a closer intercourse with his people; he did not wait for the poor to bring their feuds and their complaints to him, he went to them to find out their wants; visiting them from village to village, he obtained a deeper insight into their real circumstances, and as his

school at Secundra, near Agra. The female school attached to the Burdwan mission may be here mentioned as being of somewhat similar origin. A desolating flood, followed by a fever of great severity caused by the miasma from the receding waters, depopulated the villages around Burdwan; the poor homeless orphans, thus left destitute, were collected together, and made over to the charge of the missionaries; and thus arose a Christian girls' school, where all former efforts to educate girls at all had proved unsuccessful. Thus is good brought out of evil by Him who "maketh all things for himself."

* It properly means the country of the "two rivers;" the Doab "par excellence" is that tract lying between the Ganges and the Jumna.

own eye traced the ravages of famine in their stricken homes, his heart became more keenly alive to their necessities.

Among the many discoveries which resulted from this system of close personal investigation during the years following the famine, the one which more especially comes under our notice was the frightful prevalence of the crime of infanticide in the Mid Doab. Mr. Unwin, the magistrate and collector of Mynpooree, was the first to bring this to light. It had been considered desirable to ascertain how far the population had been affected by the famine, and, with the view of taking a census, Mr. Unwin determined to take ten villages in each Pergunnah, and selecting one house in each of these villages, to count in person every head in it. In so doing (to use his own words), "I observed what previous information had led me to expect, that no single Chohanee (female Chohan), young or old, was forthcoming."

The suspicion of "foul play" thus raised, to obtain proof and to suppress it was Mr. Unwin's immediate resolve. He at once, and on his own responsibility, established a system of watchful inspection. The village watchman was to report to the police-station the birth of every female child; a policeman was to visit the house and to see her forthwith; a month after, the health of the child was to be reported; if any illness attacked her, a superior police-officer was to see her, and report to the magistrate; and if the child died under circumstances of suspicion, the body was to be sent for examination to the civil surgeon.

So prompt and so strict a *surveillance* it was scarcely

possible to evade; and the result was, that Chohan girls began to appear in villages and families where before the birth of one had never been known. An event soon after occurred which showed beyond question the reality and extent of the success which followed these measures. The account of it, as given by Mr. Raikes, in his interesting little work, "Notes on the North-Western Provinces," is highly interesting. "There is at Mynpooree an old fortress, which looks far over the valley of the Eesum river. This has been for centuries the stronghold of the Rajahs of Mynpooree; Chohans, whose ancient blood, descending from the great Pirthee Raj, and the regal stem of Neem-rana, represents *la crême de la crême* of Rajpoot aristocracy. Here, when a son, a nephew, a grandson was born to the reigning chief, the event was announced to the neighbouring city by the loud discharge of wall-pieces and matchlocks. But centuries had passed away, and no infant daughter had been known to smile within those walls.

"In 1845, however—thanks to the vigilance of Mr. Unwin—a little granddaughter was preserved by the Rajah of that day. The fact was duly notified to the Government, and a letter of congratulation and a dress of honor were at once despatched from head-quarters to the Rajah."

This recalls to our minds the similar honor conferred on the Rajah of Murvee.

Such a recognition on the part of Government set the seal of authority to measures which received their original force from the personal influence of Mr. Unwin; and the effect was wonderful. In 1843, not a single female Chohan infant was to be found in the district; in 1845, fifty-seven had been saved; in the following year the number was trebled; and by 1851 there were one thousand four hundred and eighty girls living under six years of age.

The good work thus begun by Mr. Unwin in Mynpooree was soon taken up in some of the neighbouring districts. In 1849, Mr. E. H. C. Monckton introduced it into Etaweh; and persuaded the Thakoor families, by their heads assembled in Punchayut (or council), to undertake the abolition of the practice. One of the forms of agreement then entered into is given as a specimen;*

* "We, Peetum Singh, Bisal Singh, Bhoop Singh, Hoolas Singh, &c., who have been summoned to be admonished not to commit female infanticide, beg to state that we do not murder our female children; but, as matter of precaution, we have now settled among ourselves by arbitration, that if any of our brethren be in indigent circumstances, and have not the means of defraying the marriage expenses, we will assist him to do so. To murder female infants is held in detestation by us. The opinion prevalent, that we consider it an abuse to be called father-in-law, is false; we do not think it to be so, nor do we take offence at it. Should any one among us be guilty of such an act, we will excommunicate him, and he will render himself liable to punishment by the ruling power, and to the wrath of the day of judgment. If at any time it should appear to the authorities that any one among us has committed infanticide, we will expel him from our society, and deliver over his children to become the property of Government. If to our knowledge any of our brotherhood should be guilty of the crime of infanticide, we will banish him from our society, and report the circumstance to authority.

"With reference to the report that we do not allow the female children to take nourishment from the mother's breast, we beg to state that it is false; should any one do so, he will be liable to the same punishment as we have resolved upon for those who may commit infanticide. As to the statement that when a pregnant woman draws near her time we send her over to the Mahratta territories, with a view to destroy the infant's life, if a girl, and after doing so the mother is recalled, we beg to say that, although this is not the fact, we have determined, as a prudent measure, that if any one among our class should send over his pregnant wife to the Mahratta territories, with the intention of destroying the child, if a girl, that we will excommunicate him.

"In regard to the marriage of girls, we have come to these resolutions, viz., that it is not justifiable for the father of the boy to cause the father of the girl to enter into such conditions as to marriage settlements as suit his wishes only before closing the nuptial contract (because, if the girl's father be poor, the marriage cannot take place, and must be necessarily put off); we, therefore, propose that the head men of the village should arrange the dower according to the circumstances in life of the girl's fa-

and it is a somewhat remarkable one, as utterly ignoring the existence of the custom, and at the same time prohibiting it under severe social penalties; it also contains for the first time, we believe, in the Doab, a direct allusion to the ruinous system of marriage expenses, and a voluntary determination to bring about their reduction.

This phase of the movement, which was first presented, as we have seen, in Rajpootana and Mairwarrah, now began to attract more notice. Mr. Robinson, the Commissioner of Agra, in reporting the measures that had been adopted in the districts of Mynpooree and Etaweh, thus records his own opinion:

"His Honor (the Lieutenant-Governor of the North-West Provinces) is well aware that the main incentive to the practice is the enormous expenses that are by custom thrown on the parents when a daughter is married; and I really believe that a law protecting the people from these expenses, and, under the cloak of the power of Government, saving the disgrace that attaches to refusing to incur those expenses, would be gladly received by the people."

Mr. Charles Raikes also, who had succeeded Mr. Unwin at Mynpooree, took a somewhat similar view. To his practical mind, the most tangible, as well as the most powerful motive for this atrocity, appeared to be the system so generally prevalent of exorbitant marriage

ther, and to this arrangement he must consent; and that whenever the girl's father receives a proposal from the boy's father, he should immediately declare that he is willing to abide by the decision of the arbitrators or head men, as to amount of dower."

This form of agreement is copied from Mr. Raikes's Notes on the North-West Provinces, p. 26.

expenditure. His opinion, however, differed from that of Mr. Robinson as to the best mode of dealing with this evil. He was disposed to look more favorably on the sumptuary measures which resulted from "self-legislation," than on those originating in, and deriving their authority from, Government enactments.

Taking such a view, he, as it were, struck out a course of action for himself, which he pursued vigorously and successfully in the Mynpooree district, and subsequently, as we shall see, in the Punjab.

His first attempt to put this system into force was at Sumaon, in the end of 1851. He invited all the leading Chohan Rajpoots, headed by the Rajah of Mynpooree—in whose house a second daughter had by that time been saved—to meet together in his camp at Sumaon, for the purpose of discussing the subject. This meeting took place on the 12th of November, 1851. It is thus described by Mr. Raikes:*

"I told the assembly that I came amongst them with no desire to exercise any authority over their consultations, and that whilst I would tell them my own opinion, I would also give them every assistance in carrying out their own views.

"The meeting resulted in the drawing up of the following set of resolutions, which were signed by the Rajah and every member of the assembly."

Here follows the form of agreement, which consisted of four resolutions, to this effect:

1st. The marriage expenses were to be regulated by

* In a letter to W. H. Tyler, Esq., Commissioner of the Agra Division, dated November 17, 1851.

a rate then agreed on, according to the grade of the parties.

2nd. If the father of any marriageable damsel chose of his own will to give more than the sum prescribed for his grade, well and good; but if the father of any youth demanded more than the specified sum, he was to be remonstrated with, and, if he persisted, he was to be put out of the "brotherhood," because, from his own avarice, he was bringing dishonor on the father of the damsel.

3rd. The insolence of Brahmans, Bhâts, Barbers, and others, who abused people for not spending large sums at marriage expenses, being the cause of needless profusion, it was resolved that, should such insolence or abuse be offered, they would seek redress from the magistrate.

4th. To prevent needless expenditure in crowded processions, only a moderate number of persons were to be invited, according to the grade of the parties.

Mr. Raikes then proceeds in his letter:

"I believe that this attack at the cause which leads to infanticide will succeed better than any more direct attempt.

"Knowing the Thakoors as I do, I fully expected that they would receive with attention any suggestion I might make, but I was by no means prepared for the enthusiasm with which these resolutions were carried. I am not generally sanguine as to the effects of engagements taken from the people by authority; but if you had witnessed the zeal with which these Rajpoots entered into the work of self-legislation, I believe that you would not think me over-sanguine when I express a belief that much good may come of their present resolutions. The reserve which generally attends any reference to family subjects was quite forgotten in the indignation with which they recurred to the absurd price (under the pretence of dower) put upon sons by the tribes who take their daughters in marriage.

"It is obvious, in a matter of this sort, that a combined effort must be made to secure success; and, from the spirit of the people, I am very sanguine that success is at last almost within our grasp."

Mr. Tyler also, the Commissioner of the Agra Division, to whom this letter was addressed, took the deepest interest in this movement, and was very desirous of extending it. With this end in view, he agreed, on Mr. Raikes's proposal, to visit Mynpooree and effect a gathering of all the Rajpoots from the neighbouring districts of Agra, Etaweh, Furuckabad (Futteghur), and Putteala, with those of Mynpooree. This meeting took place on the 5th of December, 1851. It is one which, as giving a more public and formal ratification of the steps taken at the first and comparatively local meeting of Sumaon, occupies so important a position, and is so frequently referred to in the subsequent history of the movement, that a full account of it will not be without interest.

Few who have had occasion to travel from Cawnpore to Agra will have failed to notice the little oasis which presents itself in that desert of dust. About one hundred miles from Cawnpore, and seventy short of Agra, on the banks of the river Eesun, surrounded with rich foliage and verdure, is the civil station of Mynpooree. In the midst of the large and handsome public buildings for secular use, the eye at once detects—a sight too rare in Indian civil stations—a Christian house of prayer, as perfect an English "village church" as India can boast. Its well-proportioned tower rising amid the surrounding trees, carries back the mind to some peaceful hamlet in Old England, and the charm is strengthened rather than dispelled by the correctness and beauty of the whole building.*

This picturesque spot was the gathering-place of all the neighbouring Rajpoots, who had been invited to discuss the Sumaon measures for ridding themselves of a custom fraught with so much misery and crime. A few days before, some of the more distant chiefs had come in, and pitched their camps in the shady mango groves of Mynpooree.

On the morning of the 5th of December, the usually quiet little station was full of life and bustle. All began to make for the place of meeting, which was an open space adjacent to the Court-house. There were proud Rajahs with their imposing cavalcades of elephants, camels, and horsemen; there were Talookdars (large landed proprietors), and Zemindars (smaller proprietors or village-holders), on horseback or in palanquins, with their smaller retinues, and a goodly array of poorer, but scarcely less proud, Rajpoots, in humble vehicles or on foot, all eager to take their part in the proceedings, and

* It is a fact worthy to be recorded, that Mr. Unwin and Mr. Raikes, who had thus labored together at Mynpooree in the cause of humanity, and whose united piety had erected this house of prayer, have been recently (within three months of each other) raised to the Judicial Bench in the Sudder Court of the North-West Provinces.—March, 1856.

to reap their share of the benefits which were hoped for from so wise a policy.

Everything seemed to promise most favorably, when a difficulty arose which had well-nigh scattered to the winds all the labors and hopes of the assembled magistrates, and deferred to an indefinite period the accomplishment of this good work, which, too, would have made its future accomplishment all the more difficult for the present failure. No sooner were they all invited to be seated in the tents provided for them, than all their community of interest in the suppression of a common evil was in danger of being lost in the feelings of mutual jealousy and rivalry, with which each one claimed for himself the first place in the assembly. There was no "Garter-King-at-Arms" to expound the laws of precedence; no seneschal who

"Knew
How to assign their rank its due."

Moreover, the unanimity of the meeting was further endangered by the unwelcome presence of a person named Poke Pal Singh, who came to represent a Rajah whose title to that rank could not be traced to the fountain of Rajpoot honor, but had been obtained through favor of the Company. To give a place among themselves to one who himself was neither Chohan, Rahtore, Budharea, nor even Kuchwaha, and only the representative of a nominal Rajah, was more than the haughty and high-born Rajpoots, the descendants of the Sun and the Moon,* were prepared to submit to. However, by great

* The Rajpoots are divided into two great classes, claiming descent respectively from the Moon and the Sun. See Tod's Rajasthan.

tact, these obstacles were removed; and the chiefs, who had broken off into small groups to give vent to their indignation, or had retired in high dudgeon, were gradually pacified, and were induced, by appeals to their politeness, to reassemble and take their seats in the tents provided for them, without much regard to order or rank.

"The scene," says a writer who witnessed it,* "was a very gay and an impressive one. Most of the chiefs had splendid robes, either of cloth and gold, or brocade; their attendants clustered round with arms, silver sticks, and chowries. There was the boy Rajah of Mynpooree on one side, just coming into life—a life, too, in his case, promising many cares and some dangers; on the other side was another Chohan chief, the old Rajah of Purtabneir, looking already like a mummy, but wrapped up in shawls and brocade. Then came Poke Pal Singh, and close by him, looking very haughty and somewhat disgusted, remarkable by his quaint conical head-dress, was the manly young Rajah of Rampoor, the chief Rahtore of these parts."

In the midst of these, as they sat around, stood six or seven local magistrates, with Mr. Tyler, the commissioner, at their head, assisted by all the leading native officials of the district.

For three long hours did these gentlemen go about among them, explaining, answering questions, meeting objections, until they had succeeded in persuading nearly every Rajpoot present to affix his signature to the agree-

* Quoted in Raikes's Notes on the North-West Provinces, p. 39.

ment—"the charter of their unborn children." Such a sight could not fail to strike the assembled Rajpoots. "They might well" (as says the same eye-witness) "go home and tell their families that though the government of their country was in the hands of foreigners, it was carried on none the less by men who were neither strangers to their wants nor indifferent to their happiness."

Thus ended the Mynpooree meeting. The report of it, however, spread far and wide; and the amount of good which has resulted from it time alone can determine. Some of its effects were immediately felt. Through Captain Erskine, who was the Superintendent of Jaloun, the Rajpoots of that state requested to be allowed to co-operate in the object of the meeting. Another satisfactory proof that thereby a great moral and social change was coming over the minds of these Rajpoots, is to be found in a statement made to Mr. Raikes by an influential Talookdar (or large landed proprietor) named Gujadhur Singh, who lived in a remote part of the district, and came up to Mynpooree to express his thanks for the great benefits which he had himself derived from those regulations at the recent marriage of a niece.

This statement is so characteristic, that, though rather long, it is inserted in full:

"*Cherisher of the Poor, Hail!*

"I was present at the meeting of the Rajpoots, and informed your Honor of the intended marriage of my niece. Your Honor replied that, after the completion of the marriage ceremony, I was to give you the details of the transaction. This account I now render at your request.

"In conformity to the condition of the engagement, no previous conversation (as has hitherto been customary) took place between the father of the bridegroom and myself upon the dowry, although, the bridegroom's father being resident in Gwalior, I did not conceive it possible that he would have allowed the marriage to take place without my settling a dowry on my niece.

"When I informed him of the details of the engagement, and the arrangement of Government relative to Rajpoot marriages, he, with much satisfaction and many assurances that he considered the conditions of the engagement beneficial to the Rajpoots in general, acceded to the marriage without reference to the dowry. I, according to my means, willingly gave the bridegroom's father, on the day of the espousal (Suggun), and on the day when the nuptial gifts (Zeeka) were presented, four hundred rupees in cash, with three horses and a camel. I also gave two hundred rupees in cash, and two horses, on my threshold (Durwaza); and one hundred rupees in cash at the moment of giving away my niece (Kunyadan).

"By your favor and kindness the marriage expenditure amounted to only seven hundred rupees, and the bridegroom's father was pleased. Another ceremony (Raisin paldug), which generally costs five hundred rupees, I dispensed with, not considering it necessary to expend money on it.

"The above arrangements have been effected by the kind intervention of Government (*i. e.* the magistrate); and the marriage has taken place with little expense.

"In former days I spent 17,000 rupees (1700*l.*), besides the gift of horses, on the marriage of my sister, the heavy expenses of which still distress me.

"At the marriage of my sister, the Bhâts and Fugeers made a great disturbance, and annoyed me much. On this last occasion the Thannadar, at my request, gave his assistance, and by his authority many Bhâts were excluded. I presented to a few old Bhâts ten or twelve rupees, and sent them away happy. The father of the bridegroom, too, was not subjected to annoyance by the Bhâts. Formerly, the whole dowry that he received was spent upon them; but this time he did not give anything, and the dowry was so much gain.

"There is one circumstance for which I am more indebted to you than for any other kindness—viz., the discountenancing and preventing the custom formerly in practice among the Bhâts, of carrying and dancing about dolls fixed on long poles, and the filthy terms of abuse often applied by them to the parents of the young couple.

"What was requisite I have intimated to you. May the sun of your prosperity and good fortune continue to shine.

"The petition of your humble servant, Koonwar Gujadhur Singh. Dated 20th June, 1852. Mouzah Ourasur, Mustufabad."

In order to keep alive the feeling thus aroused, and to disseminate still more widely the principles of the Mynpooree regulations, Mr. Raikes, at the solicitation of

Mr. Thomason, Lieutenant-Governor of the North-West Provinces, drew up a Letter on the subject, addressed to the whole Rajpoot race of India. It was published in Hindee, and thousands of copies of it were circulated throughout the provinces. "It must be judged of" (says a writer in the Benares Magazine for June, 1852), "not by European, but by Oriental rules of composition, and as addressed to men who, though soldiers by profession, were mere children in intellectual development." It is so remarkable, as presenting a body of good English common sense, clothed in Indian idioms, and adapted to Indian ideas, that we shall extract largely from it,* as being the best exposition of the whole bearings of the question with which we have met.

Indeed, the Hindee original, of which this is a rather free translation, has been pronounced by the best scholars to be a model of idiomatic address:

"TO THE RAJPOOTS OF INDIA.

"This letter is written by me, Charles Raikes, Magistrate of Mynpooree, to the Maharajahs and Rajahs, and men of rank and landed property, of the Rajpoot race. I ask you to read, examine, and understand my letter, and act upon my advice.

"*Objects of the Letter.*

"In the ancient records of the Hindoo race, such as the Mahabharuth, Pirtee Raj Raisin, Alkund, Bikram

* It was the composition of a native, to whom Mr. Raikes suggested his ideas, and explained his meaning and object; in fact, gave the form and subject-matter, which his native friend embodied.

Bilas, and other annals, the power, valor, and generosity of the Rajpoot races are frequently celebrated.

"At the present time, too, their royal possessions, renown, and courage, are well known.

"In short, the fame of your race has spread far and wide.

"I have known you long and liked you well, and am acquainted with your customs; no wonder, then, if I wish you happiness and prosperity. But without questioning your good qualities, I must remind you of one great fault in your habits.

"You spend vast sums of money in marriage expenses; and the consequence is, many chiefs have been ruined, and from rich men have become beggars.

"It has given me much pain to see ancient families thus destroyed by foolish extravagance, and thrown into perpetual poverty.

"I proceed to remind you of the evils of profuse expenditure.

"*The Evils of Profusion.*

"It is a sad act of folly to throw away upon a temporary gratification money which has been obtained not without labor and industry; money which might add so much to your own comfort, and to the assistance in difficult times of your relatives and friends.

"To make a bonfire of your goods in order to increase your dignity, or to give your wealth to minstrels and beggars, is like the act of the drunken man, who, in order to keep his clothes in greater security, takes them out of his house and puts them in the oven.

"Think of this:

"*Prodigality causes Ruin.*

"Again, the man who borrows money to squander it on flatterers and parasites will soon lose both his honor and his property.

"Consider the debtor's case. Penniless and poverty-stricken, every man looks upon him with contempt. Nobody trusts or honors him, and when his wealth is gone, he spends his days in remorse. He is like a bee robbed of his honey, who rubs one leg against the other regretting lost sweets.

"The worst of all is, that after the prodigal is ruined, his former flatterers who eat his substance point at him, and say, 'Look and see what comes of dissolute living!' Such is the way of parasites:

> "'Whilst plenty remains, they eat and grin,
> But run from the house when hunger comes in.'

Let not wise men then, for the sake of the passing applause of interested sycophants, throw away the hardly-earned acquisitions of laborious years.

"To be provident is the part of a sensible person; to be improvident is the mark of a fool.

> "'The good man acts, but thinks before;
> The fool reflects when action's o'er;
> Wisdom to beauty lends a grace;
> But folly wears a sullen face.'

"*Loss of Land.*

"Perhaps some of my Rajpoot readers may say—'Money is but dross; I have spent it, and will earn more.' Not so fast, my friend. Mind, if you lose your money, your land does not go after it. When you have spent your money, and dissipated your other property, the chances are you will come down upon your land. It is an old saying—

"'When the bed breaks we fall upon the ground.'

"When once a taste for profuse expenditure has come over you, then away you go to some banker, and pledge or sell your land to him. Alas! your land! That land—

"'On which your grandsires shed their blood,
And cherished long through frost or flood:
The land which lent you titled fame,
And marked you with the Rajpoot's name:
Where stands your father's castled home,
Where lakes, with lotus half o'ergrown,
With trembling smile give back the trees
That glisten in the morning breeze:
Where shaded well, and sacred dome,
Alike remind you, "This is Home!"
The land which to its fruitful breast,
Ten thousand living lips has prest,
And fed with countless sugared stores
The ant that creeps, the bird that soars;
Whence nobler man or humbler beast
Still crop their never failing feast.
Nay, yield your purse, your goods, your breath;
But, Thakoor, keep your land till death.'

"A Thakoor without land is a Chakur; and, remember, when once your land is sold to another, the purchaser will say to himself—'This Thakoor belongs to the land, and will stick to it if possible; we must put him out of the way.' And such efforts will be made to get rid of the former owner, that the Thakoor, if he can't get into an ant's-hole for refuge, will be obliged to fly the country. Then the former chief will have to sound his own praises. If, by good luck, anybody believe him to be a Thakoor, he may get two rupees a month, and turn 'orderly,' and do all sorts of dirty work. I have seen scores of such

Thakoors, who eat the bread of penitence. But it is too late. They might as well water withered crops, or run away after the highway robber has carried off all their property.

"*Some Account of the Evils caused by Mobs of Beggars at Weddings.*

"Owing to the sums squandered on marriage occasions, hundreds of Bhâts, Jagas, and other vagabonds assemble and worry the wedding-folk (*i. e.* the parents of the bride and bridegroom) for money. Rich men manage somehow to satisfy these harpies, but as for poor men, they are driven to their wits' end.

"If the beggars are not satisfied, they get abusive, make up effigies,* and think nothing of calling the marriage master a knave, or a rogue, or worse names still.

"I will now tell you how these beggars killed a man the other day.

"*More about Beggars.*

"Last year, in my district, a respectable man was about to give his daughter in marriage. He had paid all the customary fees to the best of his power, and had not forgotten the beggars. But when will such wretches be

* These harpies, when a wedding is to take place, assemble from all sides, some coming ten or fifteen coss. They take up their post outside of a village the night before the procession sets off from a bride's house; when that comes by, every man amongst them, every follower of theirs, and every horse's foal, and even every dog, must be fed to the amount of a rupee. If the bridegroom's father demur, he is hustled, laid hold of, has dust thrown upon him, until at last he compounds by a considerable payment. If he fail to satisfy the Bhâts, then a bundle of rags is made up into an effigy, named after the master of the wedding party, stuck on a spear, and, with blackened face, exposed to every insult. See Report, p. 10.

satisfied? They began to press the unfortunate master of the feast, who declared he had nothing left to give them. These stony-hearted mendicants would take no denial, and at last they murdered the poor man, because he could fee them no longer.

"In that house, instead of a wedding, there was a funeral.

"And these vile beggars had a rope tied round their waists instead of a purse full of money. They were dragged away to the magistrate, and are in gaol to this day.

"But think of all the misery here caused by the abominable custom of squandering money at weddings.

"'From bitter trees you may expect bitter fruit.'

"Now, if you, the heads of Rajpoot families, would unite to put down these bad customs, it would be easy for you to do so. A wise man will not bear a grievance which can be remedied. A worthy man discriminates between good and evil; he rejects the evil and chooses the good.

"I will now tell you what the men of my district have done to remedy the practices above mentioned."

After this follows an account of the meeting at Sumaon, and the copy of the agreement, and how the agreement was ratified at the Mynpooree meeting, with an allusion to the ancient records respecting Jye Singh's measures, and those more recent ones of Colonel Hall at Mairwarrah, the substance of which has been respectively given in its proper place.

The letter then concludes in the following manner:

"*The Ending of the Letter.*

"And now I must conclude this letter. But first I may tell you that the Honorable the Lieutenant-Governor was pleased to express his approbation of the resolutions drawn up at the Mynpooree meetings; and letters were addressed, to express his Honor's satisfaction, to the Rajah of Purtabneir, the Rajah of Rampoor, the Rajah of Mynpooree, and Rao Bhowanee Singh.

"A circular order has since been issued in this district of Mynpooree by the magistrate, that all Bhâts who crowd and press upon the wedding processions more than is agreeable to the parties concerned, shall be removed by the police, and the Bhâts have been registered and exhorted to give up begging, and take to honest labor.

"*A Parting Word of Advice.*

"It remains now for you to whom this letter is sent, to address yourselves to the work of reform. I hope that you will carefully read over the resolutions to which so many of your brethren have agreed, and decide to take similar engagements upon yourselves, if opportunity offers. Thus your honor and good name will be maintained.

"If not, Thakoors will become beggars, and beggars will become Thakoors. Be wise, then, unite together, and with one effort dispel the evils which beset your race. It may seem hard at first to break through long-established custom; but when once you fling off your fetters, the countless blessings of liberty will appear; you will be esteemed the liberators of your race; and of one thing you may rest assured, that wherever the British power extends, your efforts will be encouraged, and your motives will be appreciated.

"Mynporee, August, 1852."

Soon after the publication of this letter, a call to a higher post removed Mr. Raikes from Mynpooree to the Punjab, but the flame he had kindled among the Chohans was sedulously fed and kept alive by his successors. Although we are unable here, as in the Allahabad measures, to trace the onward steps of this movement, we rejoice to be able to announce that, in the end of 1855, there were 2530 Chohanee girls alive where, in 1842, "no single Chohanee, young or old, was forthcoming." "I never go" (says the present magistrate, Mr. Cocks), "into a Chohan village, but the fathers bring me their girls to look at, and seem proud of having them."

In the preservation of these little ones may Mr. Raikes find the realisation of his most sanguine hopes, and the welcome assurance that his "fruit remaineth."

CHAPTER VII.

EFFORTS IN THE AGRA DISTRICTS.

Agra—Mr. M. Gubbins discovers the crime among the Bhudoriah Rajpoots—Enforces a most rigid system of surveillance over suspected villages—Presents medals to daughters reared in suspected families—Success apparent—Its permanency doubtful.

BEFORE proceeding to trace the subsequent labors of Mr. Montgomery and Mr. Raikes among the various "daughter-slaying" races of the Punjab, where, by a happy combination, they were brought together in 1853, we are happy in having to notice another instance of anti-infanticidal zeal in the Agra Divisions.

Mr. Martin R. Gubbins, who was magistrate of the Agra District,* had his attention directed to the existence of this crime within his jurisdiction in the beginning of 1851. He was informed, he says, by one Syud Abdool Hakeem, at that time manager of the Maafee† estate of the Rajah of Bhuddawur, that in many villages comprised in that Rajah's jagheer, "female infanticide was notoriously practised to such an extent, that scarcely a girl was ever allowed to live."‡ This information was fully

* Every division, under its commissioner, is subdivided into districts under their respective magistrates and collectors.

† Maafee means "free or exempt."

‡ See Selections from Records of Government of North-West Provinces, No. 15, containing the very valuable

confirmed by the most experienced native officers of the district, whom Mr. Gubbins consulted on the subject, and from their concurrent statements it appeared that the prevalence of the inhuman custom in some quarters was a matter of notoriety.

Anxious to carry his investigation to the fullest extent, Mr. Gubbins adopted the following plan, as the one which seemed to him most likely to elicit the truth. While marching through the Pergunnah of Bah Pinnahut, the one in which it was represented to him that the crime was most prevalent, his practice was to summon a few of the leading Zemindars of the neighbourhood, and, calling them in separately into his tent, to seat them by his side, and to take down their depositions, in the absence of others. Some of the information thus obtained was most valuable. One man pointedly observed: "In the Albheya villages the existence of the crime can be proved by the fewness of the daughters. If they do not kill them, what has become of them?" Another, when asked particularly whether the Konwur clan of Bhudoriahs killed their female infants, replied, "I never heard of the marriage of a daughter in any of the Konwur villages; I therefore suppose that they kill them." A third, when pressed with questions regarding the reputed practice among various clans, closed the subject with this remark: "Sir, most of the villages practise it more or less; what is the use of further questions? Count the boys and girls, and you can decide the question yourself."

The result of this investigation was to satisfy Mr.

memoranda of Mr. Gubbins on the subject of infanticide, from which source all our information has been obtained.

Gubbins that the crime was very prevalent among the three higher clans of the Bhudoriah Rajpoots, the Albheyas, Kooleyas, and Konwurs, but that it was not practised to any extent by the rest of the tribe.

On the subject of marriage expenditure, Mr. Gubbins was led to believe that the system of demanding exorbitant dowers did not prevail among that branch of Bhudoriahs, that it was not essential to Rajpoot marriages, and was only indulged in when men were not content with equal* alliances. The actual expenses attending the celebration of a marriage (Shadee) were not so great as to be burdensome, but the real tax was the Buddun (which is virtually the dower), the money paid by the girl's father to the father of the bridegroom before closing the contract for the marriage; this appeared to have no existence among the mass of the Bhudoriah Rajpoots of the Agra District, who were, generally speaking, content to seek out husbands for their daughters among the neighbouring clans of equal rank; but the Albheyas, and such as were too proud for such alliances, and, therefore, would be obliged to seek for sons-in-law among the distant and more expensive families of Rujwarra, and those still more costly of Rajpootana, must pay for the same; in their case the Buddun would of necessity be heavy, and, therefore, to avoid it, and, at the same time, to save the honor of their house, they destroyed their daughters.

Again, the Bhâts, &c., seemed to be less influential and less rapacious in that district; the fees paid to them, he

* *I. e.* equal in birth, and also in circumstances of life.

says, "form an inconsiderable item, and fall, not on the bride's, but upon the bridegroom's family, and their demand is not pressed with any such importunity or extortion as to require repressive interference."

On these data Mr. Gubbins came to the conclusion, in which he was supported by his native officials, that the most effectual mode of suppressing this crime would be to exercise a most close and strict supervision over all the villages which were suspected of practising it. The plan of operation which he at once decided upon, and first put into force in April, 1851, with some slight modifications and amendments subsequently introduced, may be thus briefly described:—The police-officers of the different Pergunnahs were instructed to prepare lists of all the villages which, according to common report, were open to suspicion. A very careful census of all the boys and girls under eleven years of age, showing their number, caste, and clan, was to be then made out. The head man of any accused village was to be put, as it were, on his defence; persons of other castes living in the same or neighbouring villages, were to be called in as witnesses, to establish or disprove such imputations. If, at length, the magistrate was satisfied, with the combined testimony of "fama clamosa," and the census showing an otherwise unaccountable disproportion between the children of the two sexes (taking into consideration the number of marriages within the preceding five years), that infanticide must be practised there, he placed the name of the village on his "suspected list" for preventive treatment.

The system of preventive measures adopted in the

case of every village when once placed on the "suspected list," is thus given in Mr. Gubbins's own words: "On the occasion of a birth in a Thakoor family, the village Dayee (midwife) is summoned, and, after her services have been completed, she reports the occurrence to her relative the Bullahur (constable); he informs the Chowkeedar (watchman), who causes the necessary entry to be made in the Putwaree's (village revenue collector) diary, and, if the birth of a girl, reports the event to the Thannah (police-station)."*

On the third or fourth day, the Chowkeedar, accompanied generally also by a Burkundauze (policeman) from the nearest police post, proceeds with one of the head men of the village and the Dayee to the door of the Thakoor's house, to make inquiry after the infant. The Dayee goes within, and, on her return, reports the condition of the child, adding that the mother has nursed it, when all depart, and a note to that effect is entered in the Putwaree's diary. The nursing of the infant by its mother is, among the Bhudoriahs, considered a point of much importance; for they will not (or very rarely) kill a child which has once drawn sustenance from the mother's breast.†

Thus its main feature is the immediate and compulsory registry of births and deaths of female infants in the Thakoors' families; the head man of the village, each

* To convey to the English reader a tolerably clear idea of the respective functions of these officials, it will be only necessary to say that they correspond, as nearly as may be, with those of our English myrmidons of the law; the Bullahur of the village much resembles our old parish constable; the Chowkeedar and Burkundauze (two characters introduced under our English rule) are almost identical with the "town" and "rural" police.

† Mr. Gubbins's Report, par. 28.

Thakoor individually, the village Putwarree, the Chowkeedar, the Bullahur, and the village Dayees, or midwives, are required to aid in this registry.* Here are six collateral and mutual securities, each of them bound by engagements to that effect, concerned in effecting this registry; and over these, as a still further check, are the local police-officers, whose duty it is to exact the regular fulfilment of these respective engagements; to test and examine the monthly and half-yearly returns of births and deaths, and to report them to the magistrates.

A more rigorous system it would be scarcely possible to devise.

One other feature of this system, and, to our mind, the most attractive, deserves notice: it is the presenting medals† to such children as should have been preserved in "suspected" families. Mr. Gubbins caused a number of small medals to be struck, bearing, in the Hindee character, the inscription—"God thy Preserver." One of these, attached to a small silken cord, was given to each female Rajpoot born in the suspected villages in the Pergunnah of Bah Pinnahut;‡ and was to be worn by her till her marriage or her death, when it was to be returned. The object of this medal was twofold: as a tangible record of the infant's birth, ensuring, should it

* "To carry out this system, it is necessary that the principal agents, viz., the Putwarree, Chowkeedar, and Bullahur, should be both efficient for their duties, and also directly under the influence of the magistrate and collector.

"In Agra both these conditions obtain."—Mr. Gubbins's Report.

† It is a common custom among the Hindoos to suspend a small coin or medal round the necks of the children as an ornament, or still more frequently as a charm.

‡ These medals were only distributed in Bah Pinnahut Pergunnah, where the crime was most prevalent.—Mr. Gubbins's Agra Police Report for 1852, par. 10.

die, a like record of its death; and as an emblem of the state's "protection of the child while living."

The immediate result of these measures was certainly very satisfactory. To give one instance, in a single village (Futtehpoora), in April, 1851, only two girls were alive in thirty Rajpoot families; and their lives had been preserved under very peculiar circumstances.

One of these belonged to Inrut Singh Thakoor, and had been preserved in obedience to a vow made by the father, after losing two sons successively, that he would preserve his next child, whether it was male or female. The second girl was the daughter of Gopal Singh Thakoor, and had been preserved by the accident of her mother having been absent on a visit to her own family in Oude when the child was born.* In this village, in December, 1853, Mr. Gubbins found no less than eleven girls under two years of age, who with their mothers were collected at the house of one of the principal Albheya Zemindars, where Mrs. Gubbins visited them, and distributed presents among them. In other villages there was a similar increase. It appeared, from the last year's returns from the suspected villages, that the increase of the number of girls in two and a half years was 75 per cent. The increase, as might have been expected, was the greatest in those villages in which the crime had been most prevalent. Taking forty-two of these villages which were believed to have been most addicted to the crime, it appears that between May 1st, 1851, and January 1st, 1854, the average increase of female children

* Mr. Gubbins's Infanticidal Report, par. 10.

under eleven years of age was not less than 137 per cent.; and that in some particular villages it exceeded 600 per cent., and in one village the increase reached to 850 per cent.*

So successful was the system under Mr. Gubbins's supervision.

It will be at once observed how marked a difference there is between the systems introduced into the two adjoining districts of Agra and Mynpooree. The essential characteristic of the one was compulsory enactment, that of the other self-legislation. The one based on the principle of strict registry of births and deaths, through the agency of Government subordinates and menials; the other on that of voluntary reduction of expenditure at marriages. The one looked to rendering the crime impossible, by enforcing the most rigorous *surveillance* for its prevention; the other to rendering it unnecessary,† by removing the most powerful motive to its perpetration.

In drawing the comparison between these two systems, we cannot refrain from expressing our opinion that the one introduced by Mr. Raikes at Mynpooree is best calculated to influence the masses, and to carry with it the stamp of popular approbation. Mr. Gubbins's method, on the other hand, within certain limits, and if not pushed too far, is practical, and has proved itself effectual for the suppression of the evil against which it is directed. Either course, if carefully watched, cannot fail to confer

* Mr. Gubbins's Infanticidal Report, par. 10.

† This refers, of course, only to the necessity which the Rajpoot fancies himself to labor under for the preservation of his honor.

benefits upon the people. The latter will affect localities, but the former may influence nations.

On the whole, therefore, we give the preference to the Mynpooree plan (as it is commonly called, though it has recently received a far wider adoption in the Punjab), because its tendency is to elevate and improve the people rather than to supervise and coerce them. At the same time, it is impossible to follow Mr. Gubbins in the prompt elimination and zealous enforcement of his measures, without heartily rejoicing in the success of an earnest magistrate, who would not allow evil to stalk through the land unfettered and unreproved.

CHAPTER VIII.

THE PUNJAB: ITS INFANTICIDAL RACES.

The Punjab: its geographical and civil limits; its "daughter-slaying" races—The Rajpoots of Kangra and Jummoo, and the Munhâs—The Sikhs—Gooroos Nanuk and Govind Singh—The Bedees descended from Nanuk, the Sodhees from Govind Singh—A tradition of the origin of infanticide among them—Other motives assigned—The rival races of "Manjha" and "Malwa" Sikhs—The Burars among the Khutrees—Lahoreen and Sureen feud—The Gosacens—Moyal Brahmans—Pure Pathans of the Derajat—Spurious Mahomedans—Gonduls of Shahpore, and Doghurs of Ferozepore—The Meerasees: their character and evil influence.

THE Punjab, or, as it literally means, the land of the "five waters,"* which constituted the Sikh kingdom of our

* The "five waters or rivers" which have given the name of Punjab to this country, are the Sutlej or Hyphasis of ancient history, the Ravee or Hydroates, the Chenab or Acesines, the Jhelum or Hydaspes, and the Indus. To these must be added the Beeas, which, though only a minor stream, and a tributary of the Sutlej,[1] formed the boundary of the Sikh country subsequent to 1846. The several "Doabs," or tracts of land lying between two rivers (like the ancient Mesopotamia), are thus distinguished: The Jullundhur Doab, so called from the chief city which it contains, and known also as the Trans-Sutlej States, in contradistinction to the Cis-Sutlej States, or those Sikh chiefships on the Bengal side of the Sutlej, lies between that river and the Beeas; next to the Jullundhur Doab, and lying between the Beeas and Ravee, from the initials of which two rivers the name is formed, comes the Baree Doab; that between the Ravee and the Chenab is, according to the same arbitrary plan, called the Rechua Doab; the next, formed by the Chenab and Jhelum, is on the same principle called the Juch, or sometimes, by transposition, the Chuj Doab; and the most western, between the Jhelum and the Indus, the Sind Saugor, or "Ocean of the Indus."

[1] It appears that by some authors the name Hyphasis was anciently applied to the Beeas branch as well as to the Sutlej itself. Pliny, however, calls that part of the Sutlej above its junction with the Beeas, the Hesudrus.

old ally Runjeet Singh, is that triangular tract of country lying between the Sutlej and the Indus, the apex of which is formed by the junction of these two rivers at Mithunkote, below Mooltan, the base resting on the range of the Thibetan mountains. The term, however, admits of different applications. For instance, when used to describe that territory which was annexed by the English, after the battle of Goojrat (the crowning victory of the "Punjab campaign"), in 1849, it is confined to that portion of Runjeet Singh's old kingdom which lay between the Beeas and the Indus, now technically called the Punjab Proper; for the Jullundhur Doab, lying to the left of the former river, between it and the Sutlej, and also the valley of Cashmere, had been lost to the Sikhs in 1846, when, as a penalty for crossing the Sutlej in violation of existing treaties, and also as a security to ourselves, as well as partial compensation for the expenses incurred in the "Sutlej campaign," they had been confiscated by the English Government, the Jullundhur Doab being retained under our rule, and Cashmere made over to Gholab Singh, who held the adjoining Raj, or Royalty, of Jummoo. On the other hand, the term Punjab, when applied to the present civil administration, of which Lahore is the centre, includes a far wider range, comprehending, on the north-west, that strip of land lying beyond the Indus up to the base of the Kabul and Sooliman mountains, called the Derajat, and extending in a south-easterly direction to the banks of the Jumna, embracing the several Sikh chiefships of Umballah, Thaneysur, the Hill States, &c. It is in this widest sense that we shall have occasion to use the term in the following pages.

This country presents a most varied ethnological aspect. Here are found men of all creeds and classes—Hindoo, Sikh, Mahomedan, &c.; here are royal Rajpoots, imperial Pathans, priestly Bedees, hybrid Doghurs, and, most abundant of all, the fat yeomen and tillers of the soil. An investigation of the original location of these races, and of the political convulsions which have scattered them over this part of India, would form a most interesting subject of research, but would involve too long a digression to be admissible here; it will be enough to notice so much of their peculiarities of race and faith as may be necessary to explain and account for their complicity in this unnatural crime of infanticide.

To begin with the Rajpoots, of whom we have already heard so much. The successive invasions from Asia, which have scattered the greater portion of these ancient warrior tribes over the sandy plains of Central India, appear to have driven their more northern brethren into the fastnesses of the Himalayan range. First in rank as in numbers among these Rajpoots of the Punjab Hills, are the Kutoch tribe; their existence as a royal race is of great antiquity; they are mentioned by the Greek historians of Alexander's expedition, and spoken of by Ferishta, as ruling in Kote Kangra,* in the days of the Canouge dynasty; and among all the revolutions which time and war have since made in this country, their social position

* The "Mountain Kings" on the north of the Punjab are referred to by the Greek historians of Alexander's expedition more than three hundred years before the Christian era; and Ferishta, in his introductory chapter, narrating the exploits of a former king of Kundoj, who overran the hills from Kumdon to Cashmere, subduing five hundred petty chiefs, distinctly alludes to the Rajah of Nugurkote, or "Kote Kangra."—Barnes's Kangra Settlement Report, p. 20. See also Dow's History of Hindostan, Introduction.

has undergone little change. The headship of all the pure Rajpoots of the Hills, from the Sutlej to the Ravee, has always centred in the house of Kangra. From hence many of the local tribes trace their descent. The Soodoos of the Juswan valley, and the remote Indowreeas, alike claim to be offshoots from the parent stem of Kutoch. Across the Ravee to the north are other Hill Rajpoots, who look to Jummoo as their head; from whence they derive their generic name of Jumowal.* They are somewhat inferior to those of Kangra, though recognised as the chief of the Rajpoots in their own district.† The Court of Runjeet Singh furnished a most striking proof of the tenacity with which the Kutoch of Kangra asserts and maintains this superiority. Dheean Singh, the brother of the present Maharajah Gholab Singh, while the Prime Minister of Runjeet, sought an alliance for his son, Heera Singh, with one of the daughters of the Rajah of Kangra; but the proud Kutoch deserted his hereditary kingdom rather than, as he thought, degrade his house by intermarriage even with a Meean, or prince of the Jummoo stock.‡

On the same range of hills, and along the plains at their base, from the Sutlej to the Jhelum, are found another race of Rajpoots, known by the name of the Munhâs. Of these, the Hill clans and those of the plains are quite dis-

* "It is a popular saying, that between the Sutlej and the Chenab there are twenty-two principalities, eleven on this and eleven on the other side of the Ravee. Amongst one assemblage of kings, Kangra is the acknowledged head, as Jummoo is considered paramount among the dominions across the river."—*Ibid.*

† The name Dogra or Dongra is frequently given to these races; but it would seem rather to apply to their living in the hills, from the Hindee word Dongar, which signifies "hill" or "mountain," than to be used as designating any particular tribe or class.

‡ Cunningham's History of the Sikhs, p. 189.

tinct. The former, living among a purer race, at once admit their own inferiority, and save their daughters that they might become the wives of the young Kutoches. The Munhâs of the plains, however, are in a very different position. In the districts of Goordaspore, Seealkote, and Goojrat, they are at the head instead of at the bottom of the Rajpoots around; and with them, as with those of Jummoo, and the still higher Kutoches of Kangra, infanticide has prevailed. They knew no superior clan in their neighbourhood into which their daughters might honorably marry; and thus the old motives of pride and poverty prevailed, and before their combined influence these Rajpoot houses have been for generations unblessed with the presence of a daughter.

Hitherto the Rajpoots have been, with one or two exceptions, the only class among whom the crime has been shown to prevail. But the Punjab presents a new tribe, the Sikhs, some classes of whom are no less universally addicted to it than the higher Rajpoots. They are the followers of Nanuk, the founder of the Sikh faith. Nanuk was by birth a Khutree,* of the Bedee tribe of Boonjaees,

* Some apparent confusion arises from Nanuk being by some writers described as a Khutree, and by others as a Kshutreea; the one term properly belongs to the trading community, and is equivalent to that of Bunneea; the other, as was shown at the outset, attached exclusively to the second, or military order of the Hindoos, of whom the Rajpoots are at the head. When, however, in time, the power of these Rajpoots was broken down by successive invasions, and the military occupation of the Kshutreean order ceased, it is thought that a great portion of them deserted the no longer glorious profession of arms, and became traders under the slightly altered title of Khutrees. If this be the correct view, the discrepancy of the accounts of Nanuk's birth disappear. He was a Khutree, as his father's occupation shows, and was yet most probably descended from the original order of Kshutreeas.

This explanation of the difficulty is, we are aware, open to question, as shown by a very able writer in the Benares Magazine, in reviewing Campbell's "Modern India." It is very prothe son of a grain-factor at Talwundee, in the neighbourhood of Lahore. He was born in the year 1469, and in early life deserted the humble shop of his father to seek in study and retirement more genial occupation for a naturally reflective mind. The tenets of the Hindoo and the Mahomedan of that day alike dissatisfied him; and he came forward as a reformer of his country's faith. For the gross polytheism of Hindoo mythology he substituted what may be defined a high philosophic deism, and succeeded in collecting together a large body of followers, whom he called Sikhs,* or "disciples;" and these he organised under a theocratic form of polity, being himself recognised as their Gooroo, or "teacher." For many years this rapidly increasing body of converts continued to lead a peaceful, meditative life, absorbed in the study of their holy book, the "Grunth," which contained all the recorded dogmas of their founder. They gradually spread over other parts of India; a college of them was found to exist so far south as Patna.†

But in the beginning of the seventeenth century, Govind Singh, the tenth Gooroo, gave a new character to this religious community. He was a man of a naturally warlike spirit and ambitious views, and thirsting to be revenged for domestic wrongs, soon converted the hitherto

bable that in the land of the Rajpoots a Khutree, being so vastly in the minority, would not dare to put forward such a claim, nor would the Rajpoot for one moment countenance it. But in the Punjab, where the Khutrees are an important and a rising class, the case is different; according to Cunningham, who, by the way, calls them Kshutrees, they have a legendary descent "from the warrior race who yielded to Purs Ram (King Porus), and were spared by him." Here the claim may be admitted, and the probabilities seem to be in its favour.

* From Sikhna, to learn.

† Probably founded by Gooroo Tegh Bahadur. An interesting account of this college is given in an early number of the Asiatic Society's Journal, from the pen of C. Wilkins, Esq., dated March 17, 1781.

contemplative Sikhs into a band of warriors. These were the men who a century afterwards formed the flower of Runjeet Singh's army, and whose rampant fanaticism presented so formidable an array on the different battle-fields during the Sutlej and Punjab campaigns.

Of these Sikhs, the highest class are the Bedees.* Like the Seyuds, who claim a priority over all "the faithful," as being lineal descendants of "the Prophet," these Bedees rank first among the Sikhs, as being descended from Gooroo Nanuk, the founder of their sect. They form, by virtue of their descent, an hereditary priesthood. They are to be found in greater or less numbers in all parts of the Punjab: in the districts lying at the base of the Kangra hills, at Goojranwalla in the middle of the Rechna Doab, at Gogaira on the Ravee, and at Shahpore on the Jhelum, and a few at Rawul Pindee; they are also occasionally to be met with to the south of the Sutlej. But their home and stronghold is at a town named after their founder, Derah Baba Nanuk, on the Ravee, near Buttalla. So notorious has been the crime of infanticide among them, that a Bedee was generally known by the opprobrious title of Kooree Mar, or "daughter-slayer."

With these men pride, and pride alone, prompted to the crime. The fear of poverty arising from marriage expenditure would have little weight with them, as, unlike the impoverished Rajpoots, they were generally men of wealth and affluence; they held fertile Jagheers,

* The Bedees, as has been seen, had adopted as their patronymic the name of the tribe to which their ancestor, Nanuk, belonged. But it must be borne in mind that there are Bedees still of that original tribe, who are not descendants of the Gooroo, nor, indeed, Sikhs at all.

and their priestly coffers were well filled with the offerings and dues of their race. But in defence of the unnatural custom, which they did not attempt to deny, they, like the Rajpoot races, were ready with a traditionary obligation laid upon them by an indignant ancestor. The story is thus given by Major Herbert Edwardes, of Bunnoo and Mooltan fame, who, after the Punjab campaign, held a civil appointment in the Jullundhur District, and was thus brought into close contact with the Bedees.

They say that the practice was first enjoined upon their tribe by Dhurm Chund Bedee, grandson of Baba Nanuk. "He had two sons, named Mihr Chund and Nanuk Chund, and one girl, who at the proper age was espoused to the son of a Khutree, as was then the custom of the Bedees. When the bridegroom's procession reached the house of Dhurm Chund, the door was found too narrow to admit the couch on which the boy was carried, and the riotous attendants, with more than the usual licence of the occasion, proceeded to widen it by force. The incensed Bedee prayed 'that the threshold of the Khutree tribe might in like manner come to ruin;' and the nuptial rites were celebrated amidst mutual ill feeling.

"When the bridegroom and his party were departing, the two sons of Dhurm Chund, as in duty bound, accompanied them to give them Rooksat.* The weather was hot—the party out of temper—and they took a malicious

* "Rooksat" means dismissal; it English "leave" and the French has also the double meaning of the "congé."

pleasure in taking the young Bedees further than etiquette required. When the lads returned home footsore, Dhurm Chund asked 'if the Khutrees had not bid them to turn back sooner?' The boys said 'No;' and it was then that the old man, indignant at all the insults which the bridal of his daughter had brought down upon him from an inferior class, laid the inhuman injunction on his descendants, that in future 'no Bedee should let a daughter live.' The boys were horror-stricken at so unnatural a law, and with clasped hands represented to their father that to take the life of a child was one of the greatest sins in the Shastras. But Dhurm Chund replied, 'that if the Bedees remained true to their faith, and abstained from lies and strong drink, Providence would reward them with none but male children; but, at any rate, let the burden of the crime be upon his neck, and no one else's.' And from that time forth Dhurm Chund's head fell forward upon his chest, and he evermore walked as one who bore an awful weight upon his shoulders.

"With consciences thus relieved, the race of Bedees continued for three hundred years to murder their infant daughters; and if any Bedee, out of natural feeling, preserved a girl, he was excommunicated by the rest, and treated as a common sweeper.

"Through the mists of this story it seems clear that religious pride, and horror of giving a daughter to an inferior caste, and not pecuniary consideration, first led the Bedees to adopt the custom of female infanticide; for throughout the East, I believe, it is the principle of matrimonial alliances that girls marry their equals or superiors, and boys their equals or inferiors in rank.

This placed the descendants of the great Sikh teacher on the horns of a dilemma—either to abandon their high pretensions, or else get rid of the difficulty by murdering their daughters."*

Major Abbott gives a slightly different version of this legend: "One Miher Chund, third in lineal descent from Gooroo Nanuk, had a daughter whom he married to a Baree Khutree of Buttalla, a wealthy man, who treated the daughter of the Fakeer with less consideration than she considered her due, and on her complaining to her father, he told her she had better die than suffer such treatment; so she immediately followed his advice, and died a natural death. The Fakeer, however, was revenged upon the Khutree; he and all his relations were afflicted with divers diseases, and died; the Fakeer proclaimed a law that none of his descendants should ever rear a

* Major H. Edwardes's Jullundhur Report on Infanticide, from which we also extract the following account of their inhuman process:

"It is difficult to imagine how the parents of a whole class could so systematically stifle the yearnings of nature as to carry out the murderous injunction of their early teachers; and I questioned some Bedees closely upon the actual mode of their infanticide. They said that when a Bedee mother was delivered of a child, the nurse communicated to the family outside the 'Purda' whether it was a boy or a girl. If a son, great were the congratulations, but if a daughter, the mother turned her face to the wall, well knowing the sentence that awaited her offspring; and the silence of disappointment was soon broken by the elder matrons of the family commanding the nurse to put the child to death. Various were the ways in which this order was executed; sometimes the nurse stopped the infant's breath in a few moments with her hand, but oftener the object was effected by neglect, by exposing the babe in winter on the cold floor, and in summer by aggravated heat. And, as one of my informants remarked, 'You see, Sir, they are but poor little things, and a puff of wind puts them out.'"

It is commonly believed among the people that on these occasions the Bedees go even a step farther in brutality, burying the corpse with a piece of "goor" between the lips, and a twist of cotton in the hand, and reciting this couplet:

"Goor khaiea, poonee kutteea,
Ap na aieea, bhay an ghutteea."

i. e.,

"Eat your goor, and spin your thread,
But go, and send a boy instead!"

daughter to be subjected to such disgrace, but that they were to be destroyed. This decree greatly shocked his disciples, who represented to him the dreadful crime of destroying a female child, as recorded in the Dhurm Shastra; but he replied that he would take the crime of future generations on his own shoulders, and putting up his hand to his neck to illustrate his meaning, his head turned down upon one side, and remained so all his life. Instead of attributing this visitation to the anger of the Deity, they considered it a sign that all the sin of generations to come had actually lodged upon his shoulders."*

Other motives also were assigned for avoiding the alliance between the two classes. The Khutree might plead his reluctance to marry with a Bedee girl on account of her sacred character, or (as suggested by Major Lake) his objection might assume a more practical form, in wishing to avoid an alliance with one whose sacred descent raised her above the performance of any household work: "Men who find all their ideas of God embodied in a cow, may be excused if they expect every member of their family to pay for their keep."

These latter motives might have had some weight, yet it seems not improbable that they were little more than counter-objections, started with a view to retaliate on the proud Bedee who refused to suffer the blood of the Gooroo to be, as he thought, profaned by mingling with a less sacred stream in the veins of the ordinary Khutree.

* Major Abbott's Report on Infanticide in the Hosheyarpore District.

But these Bedees do not stand in undisputed possession of the priestly office; a rival claim is put in by another class of Sikhs, called Sodhees, who also, there is every reason to fear, were accustomed under the Sikh Raj, or rule, to adopt the same inhuman mode of asserting their superiority over their lay brethren. Nanuk, the first Gooroo, was of the Bedee tribe of Boonjaee Khutrees, and his descendants took their distinctive names from that of the tribe to which he belonged. The fourth Gooroo, Ram Dass, and all the subsequent ones, who were his lineal descendants, down to the last, the great Govind, belonged to another branch of the Khutrees, called Sodhees, of the Sureen tribe; and the descendants of these later Gooroos, especially those of Govind Singh, assumed the title of Sodhees, and established a rival priesthood. The Sodhees are not a very numerous class, and are generally found on the left bank of the Sutlej, and also in the neighbourhood of Umritsur. These two races never intermarried; the Bedees, denying that Govind Singh was a real Gooroo, refused to recognise the sacerdotal equality of the Sodhees, who in return claimed for themselves, as of Sureen descent, a higher and purer origin among the Khutrees than they conceded to the Bedees. They both, therefore, in order to avoid the dilemma into which their sacerdotal pretensions and mutual rivalry brought them, destroyed their daughters to save their pride.

These priestly tribes, however, were not the only section of the Sikh race among whom this crime was said to prevail. The river Myhee, which flows into the Gulf of Cambay, divided, as we have seen,* the Northern and Southern Koombees; and in the same manner the Sutlej originally separated the Manjha from the Malwa Sikhs.† The Manjha Sikhs, or the true "Khalsa" (select or chosen), are a far more warlike, proud race than those of the south, and consequently looked down on their brethren of the "Malwa" with contempt; but they soon learned to covet their more fertile lands. About the middle of the eighteenth century they began to cross the Sutlej in free-booting parties, and by force of arms established for themselves small principalities, or seignories, among the more peaceful inhabitants. Of these, the most important were the southern states of Umballah and Thaneesur. These Sikhs from the Manjha, foreign invaders as they were, retained their assumption of superiority, and would not ally themselves with the families of the indigenous Malwa Sikhs, but married exclusively among themselves, or crossed the Sutlej to seek wives among their Manjha kindred. They resorted to infanticide to a great extent, lest they should fail to procure husbands for their daughters (if preserved) out of the small field which their pride left open to them, and thus bring dishonor on their line.

Nor are these so called indigenous Malwa Sikhs free from the charge. Those petty states lying on the left of the Sutlej, comprising what is generally called the "Phoolkeean Misl," such as Putteeala, Nabba, Furreed-

* Chap. iv., in the account of the Koombees.

† Manjha, or "Middleland," around Umritsur and Lahore; Malwa, the tract to the south of the Sutlej, so called from a fancied resemblance in fertility to the district of that name in Central India.

kote, &c., belong to a tribe of Juts,* called Burars; and although it is believed that infanticide was practised among the Juts originally, in their state of Scythian barbarism, on other grounds, "from Malthusian motives,"† it would seem that those principles which suited the days of their poverty, and prevailed chiefly among their lower grades, have disappeared before the more acceptable and flattering plea which their recently-attained "pride of place" enables them, in common with the high-born Rajpoot, to indulge in. They, however, like the rest of their infanticidal neighbours, are ready with an exculpa-

* The great body of the agricultural population of the Punjab are Juts (or Jats, or Jits, as they are variously called in different parts of India). This people are generally believed to be of Scythian origin, and to be identical with the Getæ, who poured down from Northern Asia in the fifth century, and established themselves in the Punjab, and Rajpootana, and the intervening country: these men so entirely coalesced with the Hindoos around as to become "essentially Brahminical in language and creed."—(Cunningham's Sikhs, p. 5.) They long maintained their military reputation; and history records that they offered a formidable resistance to Mahmoud of Ghuznee, and Baber; but at length they succumbed, and, like the original Hindoos, many of them yielded both their independence and their faith to their Mahomedan invaders, under whom they degenerated into a state of serfdom, and retained but little trace of their original character. The absorbing power of Sikhism, however, which drew vast numbers of Juts within its influence, and placed one of this race on the throne of Lahore,[1] and others at the head of different Misls, greatly elevated them again: and now, under the protection and encouragement afforded by the British rule, these men, in common with the Khutrees, in the exercise of their honest calling, whether it be of the plough or the scales, have received an impetus which bids fair, with their enterprising spirit, to place them at the head of the mercantile and agricultural communities of the Punjab.

† Polyandry, so general among uncivilised races, prevailed commonly among these Juts, especially in the lower classes; and it would appear, according to the opinion of a very able officer,[2] who had many opportunities of studying their character, that with them it was not the cost of dowry and general marriage expenditure which rendered them averse to rear female children; for with them girls would be at a premium, and plenty of men would be found ready to pay for brides; but in their case he is inclined to attribute it to Malthusian motives.

[1] Runjeet Singh was a Jut; Jyr Singh, Kupoor Singh, Phool, &c., were severally founders of the Ghunneea, Fygullapoorea, and Phoolkeea Misls, or "confederacies."

[2] Major (now Colonel) Goldney, for some time in civil employ at Loodiana, where he was brought into contact with the Juts.

tory tradition. They tell that a certain Rajah of Nabba had a deceit practised upon him, by which his daughter was unawares betrothed to a man of the Gil tribe, accounted by the Burars as infinitely inferior to their own. The Rajah felt himself bound to complete the marriage; but he compelled all his tribe to enter into an agreement to put all their female infants to death from that time forward, to prevent the possibility of a Burar being again subjected to such indignity and disgrace. That a daughter of their tribe should be married to a man of so inferior a class, was a stain on their high lineage; to be called brother-in-law by a Gil or a Dhareewal, an insult they would not brook. Thus, although the Jut-descended Malwa be spurned by his Manjha neighbour, he in his turn comforts himself in his own pretensions to high birth; though he be low down the ladder of rank, according to his "foreign" rival, yet he holds his place on the topmost step of that framed for his own race; and he is prepared by the same inhuman custom to assert and vindicate his pre-eminence.

Among the Khutrees, who constitute so large a portion of the Hindoo population of the Punjab, there appears to be other tribes also, besides the Gooroo-descended Bedees and Sodhees, who are guilty of infanticide. A feud, as ancient as the days of Akbar,* separated that hitherto united class, and the two leading rival branches were thenceforth distinguished as the Lahoreens and

* The particulars of this feud it appears very difficult to discover; traditional accounts vary, but they agree generally in assigning it to a controversy between certain portions of the Khutrees on that which (strange to say) is at present so prominently a *vexata questio* among the Hindoos—the second marriage of widows.

Sureens. Of these the Lahoreens claim the superiority; and so bitter has been the animosity between them, that a Lahoreen would scorn to espouse the daughter of a Sureen, nor will he affiance a daughter of his beyond the limits of his own grade. Being, then, by no means numerous, and nearly half of them already blood relations, or allied by marriage,* the Lahoreens extensively resort to infanticide in proportion to the difficulty they would find in marrying their daughters. But, revolting as such a statement appears, it is not enough that these men slay their own children to preserve their pride, or their honor; there is, if possible, a still deeper blot on their character. Their assumed and recognised superiority makes an alliance with them an object greatly to be desired; every Boonjaee Khutree (and they are a very numerous body) who has a marriageable daughter, is eager to obtain for her a Lahoreen son-in-law at any price. And as they cannot all be so favored, from the comparative paucity of the Lahoreens, it is an honor sought for all the more eagerly. Of this desire for an alliance the Lahoreen makes the most in the following manner: "The Lahoreen," says Major Edwardes, "employs his advantage to demand such a dowry as he thinks proper, which no other Khutree does. Having done this, he proceeds to run it up still higher by artifice and threatened breach of agreement. He receives the first instalment, and commits the bride's father to the match; but he refuses to advance another step without all kinds of entreaties and bribes; and so, step by step,

* See the following note.

threatening to break off, hiding the bride, &c. &c., he goes on protracting the time of the final ceremony, until the girl's father sees her approaching the age when to be unmarried is impious and disgraceful, and never allows it to be celebrated while (to use their own expression) there is any Jan, or life, left in the father-in-law's body. Here alone we see the ordinary elements of female infanticide, which exist in marriage expenses, terribly aggravated.

"But it produces a second and, if possible, more abominable form of infanticide, which, perhaps, would more correctly be called murder. For the Lahoreen father, still unsatisfied with having ruined one family, and seeing hundreds of other Boonjaee daughters aspiring to marriage with the Urhaee Ghur,* too often proceeds to get rid of the poor girl he has just been paid for receiving into his family, and either systematically starves and neglects her till she dies, or else brings about one of the thousand-and-one sudden accidents which would kill all children, if kind parents were not at hand to save them. The vacancy thus created is immediately filled by another bride and another dowry."†

The Lahoreens are mostly to be found near Mooltan and Khangur; they are also met with in the districts of

* Urhaee Ghur, the Punjabee form of Adhye Ghur, literally means two and a half houses, and is applied to the Lahoreens, as still more strongly marking their exclusiveness. The Khutrees are divided into several grades, of which the Lahoreens are the highest, and these consist of four tribes; but as a Hindoo may not marry into his father's tribe, or into any family of his mother's tribe with which she may be any way connected, which in round numbers excludes half the tribe, there only remain two and a half tribes of his grade into which the Lahoreen can marry; hence the above phrase.

† Major Edwardes's Report, par. 60 and 61.

Jhung, Shahpore, Goojranwalla, and Jhelum. In all these localities it is believed that infanticide is very prevalent among them.

In the neighbourhood of Leia and Dera Ghazee Khan, and other parts of the Punjab, another branch of Khutrees, called Goosaeens, are reported as being suspected of practising this crime. But as they are originally a body of religionists, or mendicants, on whom, according to some, celibacy is enjoined, and their only legitimate mode of perpetuating their order is by adopting boys as "Chelas,"* or pupils, we do not know on what ground they are suspected.

It has been generally thought that the Brahmans stand alone among the various Hindoo castes in an entire freedom from this crime; that either a greater reverence for the Shastras, which so peremptorily forbid it, or a more wise system of marriage expenditure, has preserved them from participating in so atrocious a practice. But an exception even to this rule meets us in the Punjab. The Moyal Brahmans, who seem to be generally distributed over the Punjab, finding themselves in a similar social position to the Lahoreen Khutrees, and deviating, it would seem, from the ordinary moderation which marks the marriage expenditure among Brahmans, did not scruple to adopt the same measure for escaping the difficulty.

The Punjab also contains a considerable body of Ma-

* They retain, as a distinctive mark of their sect, the practice of wearing some portion of their dress of a rich orange color, called Geroot, and are the only Hindoos who bury their dead. See Broughton's Letters from a Mahratta Camp, p. 129.

homedans, of whom some, like most of those found in Central India, are but spurious tribes, of Hindoo origin, who, in the days of Mahomedan ascendancy, became converts to the sword rather than the Koran, while others among them are pure Pathans. It may appear at first remarkable that any Mahomedans should be suspected of practising infanticide, when the broad difference between their marriage customs and those of the Hindoos is taken into consideration. For the Mahomedan is under no obligation, like the Hindoo, to marry his daughter in childhood, nor, indeed, to marry her at all; and it is well known that among many Mahomedan families daughters are found unmarried at thirty years of age. Nor, again, as with the Hindoos, are they in the habit of demanding and receiving large dowries. Yet the existence of the crime among them admits of easy explanation. In the Derajat,* and also near Mooltan, and round the ruins of the ancient Kussoor, the classic Sangala, are found Mahomedans who claim to be descended from the mighty Emperors of the East, Seeals, Soodozaee, and Khoduka Pathans,

"Atavis editi regibus;"

with whom the same motives prevailed that prompted the descendants of the Gooroo. Proud of their ancestral

* Along the right bank of the Indus is a tract of land called the Derajat, from the word Dera, an "encampment," as having formed the encamping grounds of the famous Belooch chiefs, Ismael Khan, Futteh Khan, and Ghazee Khan, in the fifteenth century. Those camps soon grew into important cities, which took the names of their respective founders, and became the centre of extensive districts; and this tract, lying between the Sooliman mountains and the Indus, extending from Peshawur to the borders of Sindh, formed an important frontier of the old Douranee Empire.

rank, these Pathans, like the Bedees, shrink from contaminating their pure imperial blood by suffering it to flow into plebeian veins, and therefore sacrificed their daughters.

Of the spurious Mahomedans, the most notorious for this crime appear to be the Gouduls, who live near Shahpoor, on the Jhelum, among whom the system of marriage expense prevailed to an extravagant degree; and a race of Mahomedan Rajpoots, called Doghurs,* on the left bank of the Sutlej, in the neighbourhood of Ferozepoor, who are believed to have migrated thither from Delhi.† They are a predatory race, and inherit, with the distaste of industrious occupation, all the pride and extravagance of their Hindoo progenitors. The great misfortune of these tribes is, to be at the mercy of a body of men called Meerásees,‡ who are to the Mahomedan what the Bhâts and Charans are to the Hindoo.

These Meerásees, or "Doombs," as they appear to be sometimes called, are to be found in every Mahomedan family of respectability, and attached to every Mahomedan tribe in the towns and villages, where they exercise the varied functions of heralds, registrars, and mendicants. They are conversant with all the ties and relationships of the neighbour clans for generations, which they string together in doggerel rhyme; not a birth, death, or marriage occurs, but their presence is

* These Doghurs must not be confounded with the pure Rajpoots of the Jummoo Hills, thence called Dogras. For an interesting account of this race the reader is referred to "The Adventurer in the Punjab," by Sir H. Lawrence, vol. ii. pp. 204, 205.

† Cunningham's Sikhs, p. 17.

‡ The name literally means "hereditary."

considered necessary. They know all the "marriage-ables" of both sexes for miles round, and when a man wishes to contract a marriage for a son or daughter, the Meerásee is ever ready to find a suitable alliance for him. Presuming on the exercise of these inoffensive and somewhat useful functions, which they hold by prescriptive and undisputed right, the Meerásees have been accustomed to use the influence thus obtained to practise the utmost extortion on all occasions, especially at marriages; nor were they particular in confining their favors to their Mahomedan kinsmen. The Dakhila* and the Bara are the two parts of this ceremonial at which this class of men reaped the richest harvest, and on such occasions lacs of rupees have been squandered among them. To the dread of the ruinous outlay thus extorted, thousands of female infants have fallen victims.

Such were the chief infanticidal races of the Punjab; and such, as far as we have been able to discover, the motives by which they were led into the custom. With the few exceptions specified, the Bedees and Sodhees, and, perhaps, the pure Pathans, the crime may be traced entirely to that system of exorbitant marriage expenditure which had grown out of an assumed superiority of birth, until its indulgence, even to a ruinous extent,

* The Dakhila is the distribution of money among the crowd on the arrival of the bridegroom at the bride's house; and the Bara the custom of throwing money on the Doolee, or palanquin, in which the bride is carried, and the scattering of rupees among the whole crowd of beggars attracted to the wedding, who are cooped up in an enclosed space; the greater portion of this money is appropriated by these Meerásees. We will not offend the ears of our English readers by drawing a comparison, or rather contrast, between the Bhâts, Charans, and Meerásees of India and the ancient bards of Western Europe, the Danish scalds, Scottish minstrels, or British harpers.

had come to be regarded by them as essential to their position. The foregoing outline of these tribes has been given without any regard to historical order, but merely in a collective and condensed form, to render more intelligible the subsequent history of the measures to which the discovery of the crime among them gave rise.

CHAPTER IX.

MEASURES RESULTING IN THE UMRITSUR MEETING.

Sketch of English occupation of the Sikh States from the Jumna to the Sutlej—Mr. J. Lawrence in the Jullundhur Doab first openly denounced infanticide—Major Lake, of Deenanuggur, reported its prevalence among the Bedees of Derah Baba Nanuk—Meeting held at Jullundhur to effect reconciliation between the Bedees and the Khutrees—One held at Hosheyarpore for the Rajpoots of the Lower Hills—Mr. Montgomery's report on the whole subject—The result of investigation throughout the Punjab—Seconded by Mr. Lawrence (Chief Commissioner)—Forwarded to Government, and met with approval—A proclamation issued—A large meeting held at Umritsur—Account of the meeting—Agreements signed by the heads of all classes, and by the independent Rajahs—Approbation of the Indian Government.

THE retreat of Holkar with his ally, Ameer Khan, after the battle of Deig, in 1805, and his attempt to promote an embroglio between the English and the Sikhs, by inducing the latter to espouse his cause, first brought us into direct communication with that growing power, the heterogeneous elements of which were at that time being consolidated by that master-spirit, Runjeet Singh. This wonderful man, rising out of one of the minor and least important of the twelve Misls, or confederacies, of the Sikhs, had already succeeded in bringing nearly all the other Misls into a state of recognised subordination to himself; some had been entirely absorbed, others won into alliance; until, seated on the throne of Lahore, not as a delegated viceroy, either from the Great Mogul of

Delhi, or the Abdallee Afghan of Cabul, but as an independent sovereign, he had, by various means, by force of arms, or by the fear of their force, by threats or persuasions, and not unfrequently by treachery, extended his authority over all the Sikh States to the north and west of the Sutlej, and exercised in some cases, and claimed in others, a supremacy over those on the south. Holkar's retreat, followed up so promptly by Lord Lake, brought the English troops to the very banks of this territorial boundary; and their presence there in formidable array induced the Sikhs to enter into a treaty, signed at Lahore, on the 1st of January, 1806, by which Runjeet Singh, who was then only styled a "Sirdar," and his "turban brother," Futteh Singh Alhoowallea, repudiated all league with Holkar, and pledged themselves not to molest the English. Three years later, the great political commotions which were appalling Europe extended their influence even to our Indian possessions; a formidable alliance between France and Russia, threatening an invasion of India through Persia, called for the utmost diplomacy to secure, if possible, a federal defence on our northern frontier. Mr. Elphinstone was sent to Shah Shoojah, at Cabul, and Mr. Metcalfe to Runjeet Singh. The suspicious and vacillating Rajah kept Mr. Metcalfe in unavailing attendance for many weeks, until Sir D. Ochterlony crossed the Jumna, and advanced to Loodiana with a considerable body of troops: the presence of these, within a few miles of his capital, brought Runjeet Singh to reason. A treaty of mutual friendship between the two "high contracting powers," extorted partly by the fears, and scarcely less by the hopes, of the Sikh ruler, was agreed to and signed at Umritsur, on the 25th of April, 1809, and to the general terms of that treaty Runjeet Singh adhered to the end of his life. With all his ambition, he did not lack the common sense to see that his policy lay in maintaining friendship with a power before which every native state that had attempted to put itself in rivalry had sunk. Thus did the English first take up an advanced position on the banks of the Sutlej; and though the force was subsequently reduced, and strong protestations were issued against extending our territory beyond the Jumna, Loodiana never ceased to be our frontier station.

The whole intermediate country, formed into smaller states and peopled by various classes, Sikhs, Juts, and Mahomedans, though really independent, gradually came under English influence, as seeking our protection from the threatened aggressive demands of the Lahore Rajah, as the self-constituted head of the Sikh race. The treachery of Goodut Singh, of Ladwa, during the siege of Delhi and the battle of Deig, had lost to him his feof of Kurnal, which was soon after occupied by English troops; and this force was afterwards removed to Umballa. The Rajahs of Putteala, Nabba, Jeend, Kythul, &c., were formally taken under British protection in 1809, and were subsequently known as "the protected Sikh States." The important territories of the Alhoowallea Rajah, and of Ferozepore (at that time held by a childless widow), were brought under English protection in 1827,* and the latter became, in 1838, a mili-

* Cunningham's Sikhs, p. 188.

tary station. Such were the steps by which this large tract of country, lying between the Jumna and Sutlej, commonly called the Cis-Sutlej States, was gradually brought under English influence. A political agent at Umballa, with an assistant at Loodiana, under the Resident at Delhi, formed the system of local government, which was empowered to suggest and recommend, and, in some cases, enforce, any measures of a social and administrative, as well as political, character; and among those evils arising from native misrule which attracted the attention of the English officers in this department, the prevalence of infanticide would seem to have received some notice. "It appears," says one who was for some time officially connected with these states,* "that between the years 1822 and 1846 repeated proclamations, couched in general terms, expressive of the detestation in which the crime is held by the British, were issued from the Agency Office, and it is admitted on all hands that the effect has been highly beneficial—to a great extent indeed, successful."

Still it must be confessed that such general denunciations of it, though of temporary or partial effect, were not productive of any real suppression of the crime. It was, no doubt, performed less openly and avowedly, for fear of the anger of the paramount power; but in so many small states, under independent rule, the cooperative enforcement of any system of measures does

* G. F. Edmonstone, Esq., Commissioner of Cis-Sutlej States, in a letter dated May 5, 1852, to the Secretary to the Punjab Board of Administration.

not seem to have been attempted, and, without that, permanent success could hardly be hoped for.

It has been already remarked that the Jullundhur Doab, or Trans-Sutlej States, were annexed by the English in the year 1846. In this new territory, the tocsin of war against this crime was first sounded by Mr. John Lawrence, the First Commissioner of that division. His strenuous denunciations, warnings, and threats, backed by his personal communication and influence, considerably arrested its progress in that quarter, by arousing alike the fears and sympathies of the people.

Nor must we omit to mention that, among the many duties devolving on the heads of the Lahore Durbar, in their attempt to ameliorate the devastated and degraded condition of the Punjab, this inhuman crime received consideration. Instructions were sent to Sawun Mull, the Dewan (governor) of Mooltan, and to his son and successor, the traitor Moolraj, to suppress it in that district, where it was reported to prevail. But these instructions, verbally communicated to subordinates, were unheeded.

The first official communication of its existence in the more recently annexed territory of the Punjab Proper was made by Major E. Lake, Deputy Commissioner of Deenanuggur, in November, 1851. In reporting the case of a little girl, whose death was at first thought to have taken place under suspicious circumstances, he goes on to direct the attention of the Board of Administration to the frightful prevalence of the crime among the Bedees in Derah Baba Nanuk. Around that city of the founder of their family and their faith he believed it to be universal.

"It is an undoubted fact," he says, "that there are a thousand families of Bedees who for the last four hundred years have destroyed all their female offspring: humanity demands that special measures should be taken for the suppression of this barbarous and unnatural custom."* Major Lake's report was not considered sufficiently detailed and full to justify the immediate adoption of any measures by the Board; and, moreover, it was feared that the Bedees were by no means the only class in the Punjab who perpetrated the crime. Before, then, any general system could be introduced for its suppression, further information was necessary, not only respecting the Bedees, but respecting all the classes who might be suspected of the practice; and with a view to obtaining this, a circular was addressed to the Commissioner of each of the divisions of the Punjab, directing him "to ascertain whether the crime prevailed in his district, and, if so, to what extent, and to suggest what measures he thought most likely to be effectual in suppressing the practice."

The result of this general reference tended to show that comparatively few classes were free from the crime, and to impress the minds of the authorities very strongly in favor of persuasive and sumptuary measures rather than those of surveillance and coercion.

With the writer so frequently quoted,† and who himself was soon to take so conspicuous a part in the movement in the Punjab, they saw that "the evil to be

* Extract from a letter to R. Montgomery, Esq., then Commissioner of Lahore, dated Nov. 24, 1851.

† Mr. Raikes's Notes on North West Provinces, p. 11.

mastered was not in men's bodies only, but in their souls; not only in their acts, but in their motives," and to be dealt with accordingly; that in grappling with this monster crime, the only hope of permanent success lay in destroying that principle to which it owed its existence.

While this preliminary information was being obtained, Mr. Montgomery was appointed one of the members of the Board of Administration (now under the title of Judicial Commissioner); the commissionership of Lahore, which was held for a short time by Mr. G. C. Barnes, again became vacant, and was filled by Mr. C. Raikes, whose judicious and successful plans among the Chohan Rajpoots of Mynpooree it had been decided to make the model of the Punjab measures, as "being the only true way of suppressing infanticide." It will be at once understood how great an impetus the whole movement received by the addition of so much practical experience and zeal.

The existence of this crime had been first reported among the Bedees, and among them the first attempt was made to suppress it. Mr. D. F. M'Leod, who was then Commissioner, and Major Herbert Edwardes, the Deputy Commissioner of the Jullundhur District, had from the first entered with great earnestness into this subject, and prepared very valuable reports,* setting forth the whole bearings of the case as regarded the position of the Bedees and of the Khutrees generally. Having by personal intercourse paved the way for a more easy adjustment of their difficulties, a large meeting of the Bedees

* These two Reports form the most valuable part of the Selections of Punjab Correspondence, vol. i. No. 6.

and Boonjaee Khutrees of the neighbourhood was organised, with a view to their discussing the various differences which hitherto prevented their intermarriage. It did not take place, however, until after Major Edwardes had left, and it was held under his successor, Captain Farrington (Mr. D. F. M'Leod, the Commissioner, presiding), on April 4th, 1853, at Haee Tank, near Jullundhur; a spot which had especial attraction as being a favorite place of Hindoo pilgrimage. At this meeting, the Boonjaee Khutrees (out of whom it will be remembered that Gooroo Nanuk and his descendant Bedees sprang) consented to waive all their scruples, whether arising from reverence for the sacredness of the Bedee race, or from the motives of retaliation or of economy (as suggested by Major Lake); and to give and take daughters in marriage with the Bedees, reserving only the condition that their own marriage customs and rates should be retained, which, being very economical, greatly enhanced the value of the arrangement, and indirectly set the example of adopting that principle which was afterwards to be applied to all classes. At this meeting an agreement was entered into regulating the marriage expenditure in future, which was prefaced with this remarkable admission:

"It is without doubt that the Bedee Khutrees are, from time immemorial, of the same stock as the Boonjaees, and, from the period of Baba Nanuk, when the Bedees assumed the priestly office, there has been a slight estrangement between the Bedees and Boonjaees, and the bad practice of female infanticide was practised by the Bedees, nevertheless, friendship and communication continued with the Boonjaees. Under the British Government infanticide is strictly forbidden. We now all, of our own free will, and according to the wishes of Government, have given up this wicked practice; it has become, consequently, necessary for us to settle this slight difference, and to provide marriages for our daughters."*

Shortly after (April 21st), Major Abbott, the Deputy Commissioner of Hosheyarpore, effected a gathering of all the Rajpoots residing on the lower Hills. Here the question of marriage expenditure was avowedly and openly mooted and discussed, and arrangements at once entered into—a predisposition thereto having been created by his personal intercourse and influence.

In the middle of that year (1853) Mr. Montgomery condensed into a most able and interesting report the whole of the information he had received from all quarters. He learned that our efforts and influence among the races who peopled the Cis-Sutlej States and the Jullundhur Doab had not been altogether ineffectual. Our interference had certainly been felt. Men no longer avowed the practice, as formerly, nor perpetrated it so openly. In some cases a parent's tender heart, or his conviction of the enormity of the act, came to the rescue of a helpless babe, under the security and protection of English law. Thus it appeared that, even among the classes who had been most notorious for the crime, girls were now occasionally met with, and their numbers gradually increased.† Yet

* Selections of Punjab Correspondence, vol. i. p. 517.

† This improvement was most perceptible among the Sodhees, and to some extent among the Bedees also, who had already shown a readiness to lay aside their proud exclusive claims, and become contented to intermarry with the better Khutree clans.

the disproportion of the sexes remained, and the crime was still unquestionably perpetrated to an appalling extent. While, however, our rule had given so much protection and encouragement to the tender-hearted or conscientious parent, it had, on the other hand, created, or rather strengthened, another evil—the unrestrained importunity and extortion of the beggars. Under the Sikh reign, when every man "did what was right in his own eyes," these mendicants were occasionally kept in order by the fear of being beaten off by those who had the courage to make so good a use of their freedom of action; but under our rule, as it was "not lawful to beat any one," the extortion of these mendicants, emboldened by impunity, had become excessive. It became necessary, therefore, to interfere for the protection of marriage parties against these harpies. Mr. Montgomery, in reporting the result of the general inquiry, suggested that the great principle of voluntary reduction of marriage expenses, which had been so readily adopted by the Bedees and Rajpoots at the Jullundhur and Hosheyarpore meetings, should be introduced, and that the law should interpose to secure all marriage parties from the attacks of the Bhâts and Meerásees. This report was passed on to Government by Mr. J. Lawrence, the Chief Commissioner, with some valuable comments of his own. He "strongly deprecated any strict system of supervision by the police as certain to be impotent for good, and liable to be used as an engine of extortion and oppression.

"A system of espionage" (he went on to say) "is but likely to enlist the feelings of the people against our efforts, and thus furnish a powerful inducement to thwart them. If we can once get influential natives to set their faces against female infanticide, to consider it a crime and a disgrace, our eventual success may be deemed certain.

"Any measure by which the expense attendant on the marriage ceremony can be fixed at a moderate sum, proportioned to the means of the bride's family, will produce the best results. It is astonishing what large sums are spent on such occasions. People live to save money to marry their daughters; others impoverish themselves for life to outvie their neighbours. Such is the custom all over India; but it is, perhaps, carried to a greater extent in the Punjab than elsewhere. Seventeen lacs of rupees (170,000*l.*) are said to have been spent at the marriage of Konwur Nao-Nihal Singh, grandson of Runjeet Singh, with the daughter of the Ataree Chief. Eight lacs (80,000*l.*) at that of the late Rajah of Alhoowallea. The other day, Rajah Tej Singh expended a lac of rupees (10,000*l.*) at the wedding of his niece, married to the son of a poor Brahmin, near Saharunpoor. In every rank of life the Hindoo, economical and even parsimonious in every other respect, is lavish on this occasion."*

The Chief Commissioner also confirmed a suggestion which had been made by Mr. Montgomery, that a meeting of the heads and most influential men of the tribes known to practise it within two hundred miles of Umritsur should be held at that city at the next Dewallee festival, for the sake of discussing the subject of inter-

* Letter, No. 458, from P. Melvill, Esq., Secretary to the Chief Commissioner, to the Officiating Secretary to Government of India, Foreign Department, July 8, 1853.

marriage generally, and drawing up rules for future regulation of marriage expenditure.

The report and its attendant recommendation received the hearty approval and support of the Indian Government, as was communicated to the Chief Commissioner in a letter from the Secretary to the Government of India, from which the following passages are extracted:*

"The Governor-General in Council has read these papers with deep interest and much gratification. He can conceive no purer or higher source of pride for the public officers of a state than such a record as this of the wide and rapid success of their exertions on behalf of the honor of our rule in the rescue of suffering humanity—exertions which are so eminently calculated to reflect honor on the British name, and to add largely to the material happiness of the people whom Providence has lately confided to our care.

"The steps proposed by you, at the suggestion of the Judicial Commissioner, are approved of by his Lordship in Council. Concurring with you in the opinion that anything like open supervision, or secret espionage, on the part of the police should be avoided, as likely to lead to extortion and oppression, the Governor-General in Council is nevertheless of opinion that the sentiments of the Government, in condemnation of this horrible crime, should not be left to make their own way upon the convictions of the people, but should be openly proclaimed and enforced, by denunciation of certain punishment upon those who are convicted of offending.

* The entire letter, No. 3894, dated Sept. 7, 1853, will be found in the Appendix.

"There are two causes alleged for female infanticide; the one is a religious one, founded upon peculiar tenets or considerations of caste; the other is a pecuniary one, arising out of the habitual expenditure of large sums upon marriage ceremonies.

"The Government can bring its authority to bear upon both causes, by proclaiming that the destruction of female children is murder, whatever may be the moving cause of the crime, and that it shall, in case of conviction, be implacably visited with the punishment justly due to every murderer.

"The second of the two causes of infanticide can only be effectually removed by a voluntary determination of the people themselves to limit, by common consent, the expenses of marriage ceremonies to such amounts as shall do away with all inducement to, or pretext for, the secret destruction of their female children. To this end, the proposed great meeting at Umritsur during the ensuing Dewallee will materially conduce. The Governor-General in Council will look with the keenest interest for the reports (which you and your coadjutors are requested to forward) of the results of this important gathering.

"If the Government of India can in any way contribute to the probabilities of success, it will be most ready to do so."

In accordance with these instructions, the following PROCLAMATION was drawn up, and issued throughout the Punjab:

"Whereas, it has been brought to the notice of the Most Noble the Governor-General in Council, that the practice of destroying female children, either at the time of birth, or subsequently, is prevalent among certain classes of people in the Punjab, the following orders are, by direction of the Most Noble the Governor-General, hereby notified to the public, for their information and guidance, with a view to the suppression of this horrid practice, which is sinful in the eyes of God, and hateful to the authorities:

"1. Any person committing the crime of infanticide, in defiance of God and of the authorities, will incur the penalty of murder.

"2. The crime was most prevalent among the Bedee community, but some of the members have lately abstained from it. This fact has afforded great satisfaction to the Most Noble the Governor-General, and it is hoped that all the Bedees, without exception, will give up the evil practice, and follow the right path; otherwise, those families who continue to perpetrate the crime shall, besides incurring the above penalty (*i.e.* of murder), forfeit all their Jagheers and other pensionary allowances, &c., which may have been assigned to them by Government.

"3. Any person who, conscientiously fearing God and the authorities, may use his endeavours towards suppressing the crime of female infanticide, in compliance with the wishes of Government, will be held deserving of reward, honor, and title from the Most Noble the Governor-General of India.

"4. Be it known that a general meeting of high British functionaries attached to the Punjab, and of Rajahs, chiefs, and other native gentry, will be held at Umritsur, in the month of Katik (October), during the Dewallee festival, with a view to devise measures for the suppression of female infanticide. All persons desirous of attending the meeting are hereby invited to do so at the time and place above indicated."*

The tenor of this proclamation presents a striking contrast to all official documents that had previously appeared on the subject, not more in the distinct manner in which the crime is alluded to and pronounced to be murder, than in the high, pure principles on which it is reprobated by a Christian Government; principles which they avowed themselves prepared to support by the full weight of moral influence as well as legislative authority. Confiscated Jagheers and forfeited pensions were in future to follow the conviction of any member of a Bedee family, whereas rewards or honors, or even titles, were in store for such as should be most forward in abandoning the inhuman practices of their forefathers.

Such were the steps which led to that vast gathering at Umritsur, in the end of October, 1853, which for the numbers and rank of the assembly, as well as for its after-influence, may be well regarded as the great epoch in the history of the anti-infanticidal movement.

Here were assembled independent Rajahs and tributary Jagheerdars; high Rajpoots of Kangra and Jummoo, and Munhâs from the plains; wealthy Bedees of Derah Nanuk and Gogaira; Brahmans, and Khutrees, and Mahomedans; the commercial and municipal heads of every city of note, and delegates from the agricultural and

* Selections from the Public Correspondence of the Punjab, vol. i. No. 6, p. 441.

trading communities of every district within two hundred miles of Umritsur.

This meeting, as originally arranged, was to have been presided over by the leading Punjab functionaries; the Chief Commissioner, Mr. Lawrence, with his judicial and financial colleagues, Mr. Montgomery and Mr. Edmonstone, supported by Mr. D. F. M'Leod, Mr. Charles Raikes, and Mr. G. C. Barnes, at that time, respectively, Commissioners of the Jullundhur, Lahore, and Cis-Sutlej Divisions—"the first (Mr. M'Leod), as having taken the chief lead in the suppressing infanticide in the Punjab; the second (Mr. Raikes), as being the great originator of the movement in India; and the third (Mr. Barnes), as possessing greater influence with the Rajpoots of Kangra than any other person."* But Mr. Lawrence was urgently summoned to the frontier,† and Mr. Raikes was prevented attending by sudden and severe illness—an absence deeply regretted by the whole meeting, not only because he had taken so lively an interest in it, but because he was looked to as the expositor of the principle which he had himself originated, and which that meeting was assembled to carry out. The chief duties, therefore, devolved on Mr. Montgomery and Mr. Edmonstone, the Judicial and Financial Commissioners, who were supported by Mr. M'Leod and Mr. Barnes, and assisted throughout by nearly all the neighbouring Deputy Commissioners. To Mr. C. Saunders, of Umritsur, the greatest praise was justly accorded for the entire ar-

* Mr. Montgomery's Minutes on Infanticide. Selections of Punjab Correspondence, vol. i. p. 416.

† Colonel Mackeson had been assassinated a short time before, and disturbances were expected at Peshawur.

rangements, "which added so much *éclat* and dignity to the meeting."

The first day was devoted to the preliminary formation of a general committee, comprising all the most intelligent and influential Rajahs and Sirdars, with the Deputy Commissioners. By these, the principles of the two meetings already held at Jullundhur and Hosheyarpore, affecting the Bedees and Rajpoots, were discussed, and pronounced to be capable of general application; and it was agreed that they should be taken as the basis of future proceedings.

On the second day these principles were communicated by the heads and delegates to their different tribes and classes, in private conclave. The Rambagh presented the novel and striking scene of bodies of natives—Rajpoots, Bedees, Khutrees, Mahomedans, &c.—formed into separate groups, under the guidance of their own chiefs, deliberating on the most important object for which they had been brought together by their English rulers.

"Rajah Deena Nath and Rajah Saheb Deeal presided over the deliberations of the Brahmin and Khutree committees, and were both able and valuable counsellors on the occasion. Sirdar Shumshere Singh and Metab Singh, respectively the representatives of the noble Sindeeanwala and Mujetea families, Sirdar Kirpal Singh, Mulvee, and Hurdut Singh, Budanea, with Sirdar Jod Singh and other Sikh chieftains, guided the deliberations of the Jat and Sikh fraternities, and contributed greatly by their advice and countenance to a satisfactory termination. Nawab Emam-oo-deen Khan, and other Mahomedan gentlemen, presided over the council of the

Mahomedans, and appeared to take the same warm and praiseworthy interest in furthering the object of the meeting. . . . . .

"After four or five hours' close and earnest consultation, the committee handed in their several written and duly-attested agreements. In these documents were laid down well-graduated scales of marriage expenditure for the different castes and communities whose interests were concerned. In the majority of them three or four grades of expenditure, according to the means and position in society of the parties contracting the marriage, were recognised, and a maximum as well as a minimum of expenditure fixed; also all the details of charge, the gratuities to Brahmins, Barbers, and others, and the other incidental expenses of the marriage feast and procession were laid down at length."*

The third and last day of this meeting were devoted to the great Durbar, or Council, when all who had hitherto been deliberating separately were to combine together in one general assembly, and to declare publicly, as it were, "with one heart and one voice," their determination to suppress this crime. Pavilion-tents had been pitched enclosing an area of some two hundred feet in length and sixty in breadth, and capable of accommodating about three thousand people. Of this canvas hall of audience the upper part was appropriated to the English functionaries and the native chiefs, with their personal attendants. Seats for about sixty of the most important of these were arranged in the usual semicircular form,

* Official Report of the Umritsur Meeting, Selections, &c., vol. i. p. 434.

the centre ones being occupied by the Commissioners; Deputy Commissioners being judiciously distributed at intervals of four or five among the Rajahs and Sirdars, and brought as far as it was possible in proximity with the leading men in their several districts. The arrangement of so large a body of native nobles and gentlemen of every grade was no easy task; and lest all their previous labor should be rendered nugatory, and a similar dilemma arise to that which so greatly imperilled the unanimity of the Mynpooree meeting, a committee of five of the Deputy Commissioners was formed, to whom was entrusted this most difficult and delicate proceeding. Of this committee, Mr. J. Inglis and Mr. Bowring—whose former connexion with the Lahore Durbar had made them conversant with native etiquette and the rules of precedence—were the most active. Each native Rajah, and Sirdar, and gentleman was received on entering the reception-tent by one of the members of this committee, and conducted with becoming honor and due marks of consideration to the seat allotted to him; and so perfect were these arrangements, that, "though an unprecedented number of natives of rank were assembled, there was not a single expression of disapproval, disappointment, or displeasure."*

The account of this Durbar is thus further given in the Official Report:

"The business of the meeting was opened by Mr. Edmonstone, who, after a few preliminary remarks, read a translation of the Governor-General's letter conveying

* Report of the Umritsur Meeting, Selections, &c., p. 437. For the plan of the Durbar, see Appendix.

his sanction to, and approval of, the objects of the meeting; his determination to punish all who might be hereafter convicted of female infanticide as for murder, no less than his readiness to confer honorary distinctions on those who might cordially co-operate with the officers of Government in extirpating the inhuman practice. Mr. Edmonstone then expressed the anxiety with which the Government officers had watched the deliberations of the several classes on the preceding day, and the satisfaction with which intelligence of their successful termination had been received; and concluded by reading the general form of agreement, and demanding from the assembled crowds whether they concurred in the sentiments which it expressed, and were prepared to signify their determination to conform to the conditions which it recited by affixing their signatures in the presence of the representatives of Government. On a general expression of assent being given, numerous copies of it were handed round for signature, the Rajpoots and other chiefs signing.* Subsequently, Mr. M'Leod rose, and conveyed the thanks of Government to those Residents of the Jullundhur and Hosheyarpore districts, who in the previous year had taken the lead in the measures which now had been generally adopted. He exhorted all present not only to act up to the letter of the engagements into which they had severally entered, but to receive and adopt them in their whole spirit, and to omit no opportunity of manifesting their detestation of the practice, as well as of contributing to its extinction."†

* The form of agreement is given in Appendix.

† Selections of Punjab Correspondence, vol. i. p. 438.

The co-operation of the independent Rajahs who exercised judicial and fiscal power within their own Jagheers was also enlisted. Without their concurrence, all the other measures adopted would have been at least imperfect, if not futile.

The Alhoowallea Rajah, and those of Chumba, Sukeet, and Mundee, also entered into an agreement that, within their own jurisdiction, they would carry out to the full extent the principles and objects of this meeting.*

The Official Report thus concludes:

"The Commissioners are persuaded that this determination will be long impressed on the recollections of all who witnessed the interesting spectacle, and that it will have the most powerful moral effect. The natural feelings of the people have been strongly appealed to; their hopes have been excited, their fears aroused, and their sense of self-interest conciliated. Some may still cling to the notions which have been fostered in their minds since childhood; still pride themselves on their superior birth, and, for a time, continue the reprobated practice; but the fear of detection, the shame of exposure, the inevitable consequences, will gradually have their ordinary effect; and it is hardly too much to anticipate that ere the present generation die out the practice will have ceased, even among those tribes who have been most addicted to it hitherto. Whatever may be the general sense of the people as to the attack which has thus openly been made upon the custom of ages—whether they are prepared or not to relinquish that which, in their estimation,

* See Appendix.

is a mark of superior birth—this, at any rate, is certain, that the people are sincere in their desire to have matrimonial expenses restricted within reasonable limits, and certain obstacles to intermarriages between particular classes removed; and there can be little doubt that they will cordially unite in carrying out the agreement which on this head they have executed. The extravagant expenditure, hitherto considered indispensable, has certainly been the main incentive to the commission of this crime; and the removal of the one affords the surest hope of the eradication of the other, in the course of time."*

A more fitting conclusion to this account of the great Umritsur meeting cannot be found than in the words in which the Governor-General in -Council communicated his congratulations to all concerned, upon "the eminent success with which their exertions had already been crowned."

"The Governor-General in Council does not think that he overrates the importance of these incidents when he describes the result of the meeting at Umritsur as the commencement of a new social era among the people of the countries beyond the Jumna.

"The benevolence, the perseverance, the judgment and tact by which this harmonious result has been educcd from out of such various and discordant materials, are honorable in the highest degree to the gentlemen whose names are enrolled in the record before his Lordship in Council.

"To see hereafter the ripening fruit of their present

* Selections of Punjab Correspondence, p. 440.

labors will be a higher reward to them than any honor that the Government or Court of Directors can bestow. Nevertheless, his Lordship in Council desires to renew to them, one and all, an assurance of the interest and deep satisfaction with which the supreme Government has marked their efforts for good, and of the earnestness with which it will endeavour duly to represent their merits to the Honorable Court."*

* Letter from J. P. Grant, Esq., Officiating Secretary to Government of India, to John Lawrence, Esq., Chief Commissioner of the Punjab, dated Feb. 1, 1854.

CHAPTER X.

REFLECTIONS ON THE UMRITSUR MEETING.

The Dewallee festival—Men of war meeting in peace—Alhoowallea Rajah—Rajahs Tej Singh and Deena Nath—Nawab (Sheik) Emam-oo-deen—Sirdar Shumshere Singh, Sindeeanwala—Kangra and Jumowal Rajahs—Moofsid Sikhs—The Bedee Bikrama Singh not permitted to attend—Concluding remarks.

SUCH was the great Umritsur meeting of 1853. In the foregoing account we have been glad to avail ourselves largely of the language of those officers whose privilege it was to take part in this good work. Their full and lucid accounts of the steps which led to this meeting, and the circumstances attending it, afforded, as we felt, the best medium for presenting a clear insight into the movement itself, and into the deep interest which led them on to further it; yet we may be permitted to offer a few remarks on this most interesting event, before proceeding to trace out the subsequent measures which extended the influence of this meeting through the length and breadth of the Punjab. We will, moreover, trespass on our readers' patience with a short account of the most notable among that goodly array of native chiefs who were there assembled, rejoicing if our proximity to some of the scenes of their memorable deeds shall enable us to catch, before they have altogether passed away, the still floating rumours of personal incident for which history would find no place.

The Dewallee* was the occasion selected for this meeting. This festival is held in honor of Lukshmee, or Luchmee, who may be regarded as the Venus of the Hindoos, for in mythological descent and history she greatly resembles that Pagan deity, though in this festival more importance is attached to her additional attributes of being the dispenser of prosperity and wealth. On this occasion she is supposed to descend from heaven, and to enter those houses where an open door and bright illumination, inside and out, invite her auspicious presence. On such a night no Hindoo is too poor to make some brilliant demonstration of respect, in hope of gaining her favor. The Dewallee is usually a great gathering time for the Sikhs. Their holy city with its sacred tank are then studded with ten thousand lights, where, lining the margin of the vast basin, festooned from pillar to pillar, and ascending tier on tier to the top of each lofty minaret and swelling dome, their glimmer, reflected on the water below, presents a sight that goes far to realise the brightest dreams of fairy-land.

This was the festival so well chosen for assembling all the leaders of the "daughter-slaying" races to deliberate on this most important social question, with all the solemnity of association and attractiveness which Umritsur could impart to its celebration. Here, in the city which

* This festival takes place on the new moon in the month *Aswin*, or *Kartik*—September-October.

contained the temple of the fourth Gooroo, Ram Dass, to whom history assigns the honor of being its founder, and of digging* the vast tank—the "head of the water of life;" where also were enshrined the apocryphal battle-axe and Tulwar (or sword) of their warrior Gooroo, the Singh† Govind, before which the old chivalry of the Punjab used to prostrate themselves every year‡ and lay aside for a time their mutual animosities, and kindle anew the flame of their feudalism; where, not quite fifty years before, the youthful Representative of England§ had extorted from the fears and policy of "the Lion of the Punjab" the first treaty of mutual alliance, which formed the basis of all subsequent international peace until the death of Runjeet. Here, at this Kibla of the Sikh race, were assembled together, at the suggestion of the English rulers, within four years after their power had become paramount in the Punjab, what remained of the nobles and statesmen that had constituted Runjeet Singh's court.

* Or, as some say, of discovering what had been the work of the Hindoo deity, Ram Chunder. See Cunningham's History of the Sikhs, p. 48.

† The word Singh, which literally means a lion, and metaphorically a champion or warrior, was first applied to the Sikhs, and to himself by Govind (ibid. p. 70). The term has now fallen into indiscriminate use, especially in the Punjab.

‡ Year by year the "Surbut Khâlsa," or "whole Sikh people, met once at least at Umritsur, on the occasion of the festival of the mythological Rama, when the cessation of the periodical rains rendered military operations practicable. It was perhaps hoped that the performance of religious duties, and the awe inspired by so holy a place, might cause selfishness to yield to a regard for the general welfare; and the assembly of chiefs was termed a Gooroomutta," to denote that, in conformity with Govind's injunctions, they sought wisdom and unanimity of counsel from their teacher and the book of his word. "Mut" means understanding; "Mutta," counsel or wisdom. Hence, Gooroomutta becomes literally "the advice of the Gooroo."—Cunningham's History of the Sikhs, p. 104.

§ Sir Charles Metcalfe was only twenty-three years old when he first displayed his diplomatic powers; and, in spite of the fickleness and the freaks of Runjeet Singh, brought about the treaty of April 25, 1809, in the Rajah's camp at Umritsur. See Kaye's Life of Lord Metcalfe.

Palaces and forts, and strong-walled cities, that but a few years before had let loose the hell-hounds of war on this unhappy land, to slake a thirst for ambition or revenge—homes that still bore their dismal records of the internecine strife,

> "Stamped in fierce meaning on the battered wall,
> Writ in the silence of the ruined hall"—

now poured forth their inmates, no longer "in the pomp and circumstance of war," to imbrue their hands in the life-blood of rivals or of foreign foes, but

> "In garb of peace, on mercy bent;"

men of every rank, and race, and faith, to ratify a common bond, to set their seal to "the charter of their children," by which the lives of daughters yet unborn should be rescued from the talons of that demon—pride, and be nurtured and loved till in their marriage contracts ancient feuds should be buried, and new ties and friendships called into life. All this was hoped for in that Umritsur meeting.

The first to appear on the scene was the Rajah of Kuppoothulla, Rundheer Singh, the head of the Alhoowallea Misl or confederacy, accompanied by his younger brother, Koonwar Bikrama Singh. They were grandsons of Futteh Singh Alhoowallea, the turban brother* of Maharajah Runjeet Singh, who joined with him in signing the treaty of 1805.

* The exchange of turbans is the symbol of the closest friendship and alliance; on some public occasion Runjeet Singh went through this ceremony with Futteh Singh, and the latter was henceforward called his "turban brother."—Cunningham's Sikhs, p. 131.

This young Kuppoothulla Rajah, as he is called from the fief he holds, had from the first evinced the deepest concern for the success of the measures which it was proposed to adopt for the suppression of a custom, the evils of which he so well knew, and had given the fullest assurance of the cordial co-operation which might be looked for from him* when the time should arrive for maturing and enforcing those measures; and to the Rajah of Kuppoothulla much is due for the noble example he set to the Sikh chieftains on this occasion.

Another of the leading members of this "National Conference" was Rajah Tej Singh, one whose name holds a prominent place in the history of both campaigns. In the former campaign he was sent forth by the Sikh Sirdars, and the voice of the army, to take the field under Lall Singh ; and to his known reluctance to come into collision with the English—a respect for whom he had imbibed from his patron, Runjeet Singh, and his brave old uncle, Khooshyal Singh, the famous "Jemadar" —as justly as to any insinuated treachery, may be attributed the course he pursued on the banks of the Sutlej. On the termination of the campaign, when the English army occupied Lahore, he was selected for the appointment of President of the Council of Regency, which was formed to carry on the Government of the Punjab during the minority of the young Maharajah Dhuleep Singh. In that peaceful assembly at Umritsur sat this grey-headed warrior, whose word a few years before had swayed the armies of the Khâlsa, whose wishes and opinions Go-

* See, in Appendix, a letter addressed by him to D. F. M'Leod, Esq., on the subject.

vernor-Generals of India and Commanders-in-Chief had paused to consult, now little more than a private individual, with nominal rank and no power; the heirless pensioner of the British Government, with little left to connect him with his former power and pomp, save the palace of the old Jemadar Khooshyal Singh at Lahore, a princely dwelling at Umritsur, and the old fort at Seealkote.* Yet, nobly does the old man bear his change of fortune—unostentatious, yet dignified; uncomplaining, though fallen; thankful, it may be, that English rule has interposed to save him from adding one more to the countless victims of Sikh intrigue, anarchy, and massacre, and that if he be somewhat shorn of power and rank, he may yet hope to end his days in peace.

Rajah Deena Nath was also there, taking no unimportant part in the arrangements of the meeting, and greatly conducing by his influence and example to its satisfactory result. He too, like Tej Singh, had held high office under Runjeet, having raised himself by great ability and industry to the entire charge of the finances of the empire. His faithfulness to the English, though once doubtful, was found proof against the machinations of Churut Singh to involve him in Shere Singh's rebellion.

Here, also, was Nawab (Sheik) Emam-oo-deen, one who held a place of some importance among the local Governors of the Punjab. His first office under the

* Of this fort the Rajah is especially proud. While all the other Sikh forts have either been appropriated by the English Government, as Lahore, Govindghur, and Phillour, or entirely demolished, on him alone of all the Sikh chiefs the honor of retaining one has been conferred—a distinction the old warrior duly values.

English was that of temporary Governor of Cashmere. Here he attempted to organise a rebellion, and become the rallying-point of the disbanded Sikhs, and was even bold enough for a time to retain possession of Cashmere when called on to transfer it to Gholab Singh; but the Khâlsa, however disaffected towards the "Feringee,"* mistrusted the Moslemite, and his treasonable designs failed; and he only escaped the punishment he deserved by the weight of the Durbar's indignation falling on the arch-traitor Lall Singh. Two years after, however, he was able to atone for his former conduct by faithfully co-operating with the English force under the walls of Mooltan.

Sirdar Shumshere Singh, the head of the Sindeeanwala Misl, was admitted to a high position among the Sirdars, while many other members of his house found far less honored places, having failed to efface from the public mind the remembrance of the part they had taken in the rebellion. Shumshere Singh for a time seemed involved in the treachery of Shere Singh, when the latter joined the forces of Moolraj, and headed the rebellion; but the proof which the Sindeeanwala Rajah gave of his reluctant and compulsory connexion with that traitor, in seizing the first opportunity of escaping from Mooltan and seeking shelter in Edwardes's camp, restored him to favor.†

The other Punjab leaders, who by their presence and

* "Feringee" is a term of scorn by which Englishmen are sometimes called by the inhabitants of Northern India and Central Asia. It is probably a corruption of the word "Frank," traditionally preserved among the followers of the Prophet since the days of the Crusades.

† Edwardes's Year on the Punjab Frontier, vol. ii. p. 622.

co-operation helped to carry out this great social reform, were not men of sufficient note to require remark. Here were the eleven Rajahs of the Kangra group of Rajpoots, either in person or by representatives; the arranging of whom, according to their rival claims of precedence, was a most difficult task; and only the tact of the officers, who, placing all their chairs together, seated them in the order in which they chanced to enter, saved them, and spared the meeting all the evil consequences of their mutual jealousies and discontent.

Dewan Hurree Chund, also, the influential Minister of the Maharajah Gholab Singh of Cashmere, represented his sovereign, and was accompanied by the heads of the other Dogra clans of the Jummowal group of Rajpoots.

Beside the Sindeeanwala Sirdars already alluded to, whose names will be found far away from the posts of honor, near the extremities of the semicircle in which they were arranged, there were some, too, of the Attareewala and Majeethea Misls, whom the word Moofsid (rebel), attached to their names, consigned to a similar fate. Though received under the general amnesty, and partly restored to their former Jagheers, or pensioned by the Government, the part they had played in that drama of intrigue and carnage was yet remembered, and this was deemed a good opportunity for marking publicly a sense of their past delinquencies. Conscious of their political power, and strong in the goodness of their righteous cause, and believing, too, that that power might be greatly strengthened, and that cause promoted by such a demonstration of moral influence, the Punjab Government, while gladly accepting the co-operation of these Moofsid Sikhs in the great work before them, did not suffer it to be forgotten that by their former rebellion they had forfeited their high rank among their brethren, and that even an humble place in that proud assembly was obtained rather by favor than by right.

But, in speaking of those who did take part in the counsels of that day, we must not omit to notice one whose presence had been expressly forbidden, the Bedee Bikrama Singh. Political as well as social reasons excluded this man. Though only in reality the head of the younger branch of the Bedee family, yet, being a man of proud, ambitious views, and imbued with the deepest fanaticism, he had contrived during the days of Sikh misrule to wrest the right of supremacy from the youthful and more feeble hands of his cousin, Baba Sumpoorun Singh of Gogaira. This usurped supremacy had become in his hands a mighty engine for sedition. In the troublous days of the Durbar, in conjunction with the disaffected and dispossessed Rajahs of Kangra and Juswan, he had organised a rebellious rising in the Hills. This, however, was speedily suppressed; the Rajahs were seized, and the Bedee effected his escape, to find shelter with the army of Shere Singh.* After the defeat of the Sikhs at Goojrat, Bikrama Singh was included in the general amnesty, and was permitted to return to Umritsur, where he still lives, a marked man, and powerless. Thus unfavorable were his political antecedents, and the social delinquencies written against him were scarcely less condemnatory. When Mr. Lawrence, as Commis-

* Barnes's Kangra Settlement Report.

sioner of Jullundhur, first endeavoured to suppress infanticide, he appealed to Bikrama Singh to give him that support which his position and known influence commanded among his own race; but the answer given was at least evasive, if not insolent.*

It was remembered, too, that in the case of a Bedee—one Punjab Singh of Mokundpore—who had preserved the lives of two daughters, in accordance with what he believed to be the spirit of the Grunth,† Bikrama Singh, at the head of the Bedees, had excommunicated him, and caused him to be subjected to every imaginable social indignity for this deviation from the murderous custom.‡ On the other hand, it was known that in the family of the superseded cousin, Baba Sumpoorun Singh, there lived a little daughter who had been preserved, it was said, at the solicitation of Lord Hardinge, when in the Punjab, in 1846. Justice, therefore, no less than policy, required the exclusion of the proud, wily, and turbulent high priest of Umritsur, and the introduction of the superseded cousin.

By so politic a course, while the conduct of the one was publicly reprobated, the sympathies of the other, already shown to be favorable, were still more forcibly enlisted, and a new claim on his co-operation established

* He said "he had long given up intercourse with the female sex, and therefore had no temptation to perpetrate the crime."

† The following passages are given by Captain Cunningham in his History of the Sikhs, p. 385, extracted from the Grunth (their holy book), as showing its condemnation of female infanticide:

"With the slayers of daughters
Whoever has intercourse, him do I curse."

And again:

"Whoever takes food from the slayers of daughters
Shall die unabsolved."

‡ Major Edwardes's Report, par. 14. Punjab Selections, vol. i. p. 447.

by this restitution of a rank which had been taken from him by his kinsman.

The present position of the Bedee Bikrama Singh cannot be better explained than by the following incident: A son of his was lately married to the daughter of a high Brahman at Benares, and the Bedee solicited of Government permission to be present on the occasion; but, for political reasons, from the still dangerous character of the man, it was refused! This man, then, who once had worn the proud tiara of Sikhdom,—he to whom, a few years ago, Rajahs and Sirdars would have humbly offered the most costly gifts, and have strewn pearls and jewels at his feet in token of veneration, is now, within the precincts of his own Umritsur, a state prisoner at large, at the will and pleasure of the conquering Saxon.

"Æstuat infelix Angusto limite."

It was a goodly scene that Umritsur meeting! Men of every grade and faith assembled together to inaugurate a great principle,—a principle embracing every class, and which every class was eager to apply to its own circumstances, the reduction of marriage expenditure, by which dowries were regulated, mendicant Bhâts and Meerásees provided for, and the days of infanticide numbered.

Under the influence of this principle, the Rajpoot and the Pathan found their pride of birth no longer tempting them to the crime, the Bedees and Sodhees became willing to waive their sacerdotal pride, and the Khutrees their jealousies, and consented to intermarry; the Lahoreens and Sureens to forget the feuds which had separated them; and all were ready to renounce this inhuman practice; for they now saw a way of preserving their pride, their purses, and their daughters. They saw, too, that which had no little effect in moving them—they saw their English rulers, with disinterested benevolence, coming among them, not only pointing out the evils under which they groaned, but suggesting the way of escaping from them; in short, proposing a great social reform, the benefits of which they could all foresee, but which not any one of their body, nor any number of them together, could have originated, for fear of misrepresentation and abuse.

In that Umritsur meeting was rung the knell of female infanticide in the Punjab!

CHAPTER XI.

SUBSIDIARY DISTRICT MEETINGS.

Goojranwalla, Rawul Pindee, Jhelum, Shahpore, Mooltan, with their several local associations—Measures among the Kangra Rajpoots (regarding breach of contracts)—Meetings at Umballa and Ferozepore—The meeting of Jummowal Rajpoots at Budheeal under the Prince Runbheer Singh—Description of the meeting—Approbation of the Indian Government—Private congratulations of Lord Dalhousie conveyed to Mr. Raikes on the success of his measures.

So successful was the Umritsur meeting—exceeding even the most sanguine expectations as to the unanimous and cordial assent of the various classes whom it comprised—that it was resolved to extend the influence thus gained to other districts. A call was made by Mr. Montgomery, through the several Commissioners on those districts not included within the range comprised by the "Umritsur gathering," to hold local meetings for the purpose of explaining and obtaining a wider adoption of the resolutions agreed to there.

The first to respond to this call was the district of Goojranwalla, which indeed had not been without its representatives at Umritsur. Goojranwalla* lies about forty miles to the north of Lahore, on the main road to Peshawur. Of this now important city little was known

* Goojranwalla is identical with the Guseraoli of Baron Hügel.

until it passed into the family of the great Sikh ruler, whose grandfather, Churut Singh, received it as a portion of his wife's dower. Under him, in 1762, it offered a successful resistance to the Affghan armies of Ahmed Shah, when they were returning fresh from the defeat of the Mahrattas, on the great Indian battle-field of Paneeput. Here Runjeet Singh himself was born in 1780,* and here his immediate ancestors were buried. But the greatest benefactor to the town was Hurree Singh, Nulwa, the Sikh general whose fall before the Affghans at Jumrood, in 1837, so much affected the Maharajah. This Hurree Singh built the whole of the "New Town," besides erecting and fortifying a noble Baradurree for his own private residence† on the outskirts.

Here, on the 5th December, 1853, was held a meeting, which in its results was most satisfactory. Nearly five thousand men, of all grades and classes, from the neighbouring Khutrees of Goojranwalla and Wuzeerabad, to the more distant Mahomedan Raats of Hafizabad, were assembled together to consider this great social question; and the agreement was signed with the utmost readiness, the whole body declaring that they "understood and

* So little was the birthplace of Runjeet Singh regarded, either by his own family, whom he had ennobled, or his race, whom he had immortalised, that the spot where he was currently believed to have first seen the light was, a few years ago, a heap of ruins. To an Englishman (the present Deputy Commissioner, Major Clarke) was it reserved to rescue it from the surrounding rubbish and threatened oblivion; and the municipal authorities have, through his persuasion, marked the spot by the erection of a large square and bazaar.

† This building is now occupied by the Deputy-Commissioner. It is thus described in Baron Hügel's Travels, p. 253: "The splendor of the rooms in the palace did not excite my admiration nearly so much as the garden; it was the most beautiful and best kept I had seen in India."

heartily accepted all its provisions."* With what mingled feelings must those assembled Sirdars and Jagheerdars have joined in that day's proceedings! On one side of the tented canopy which covered them might be seen the walls of the city that had given birth to their great national ruler, Runjeet Singh, and the glittering dome where rested the consecrated ashes of his father, Sirdar Maha Singh, and of several relatives. Amid these monuments of former power and greatness, they were receiving from "foreign" rulers a sympathy and humane interposition which the mighty men of their own race either would not, or could not, exercise in their behalf.

On the spot where that meeting was held has since been erected a church, as if to attest that here, as at Mynpooree, anti-infanticidal zeal and Christian piety have gone hand in hand.

About the same period a meeting was convened at Rawul Pindee, the centre of that kingdom which, above two thousand years ago, Taxiles had ceded to Alexander,† and near to which tradition points out the tomb of Bucephalus; a spot associated, too, in the history of our own day with the submission of sixteen thousand Sikhs, the wreck of the Khâlsa army, to the gallant Sir Walter Gilbert, in March, 1849. Here Mr. Carnac, the Deputy Commissioner, collected together the leading Hindoos, Moyal Brahmans (who were rather numerous in that

* In favor of this theory we have, among others, the opinion of Baron Hügel, who says, p. 230 of his Travels, "From the description, as given by the ancient Greek writers, I conclude that Rawul Pindee may be built on, or near, the site of Taxila."

district), and Adhyeghur Khutrees, in order to include them in the same agreements with which their kinsmen had bound themselves at Umritsur. "The Hindoo community," says Mr. Carnac, "are well aware of the light in which the crime is viewed, and the interest evinced by Government in its suppression; moreover, the feeling of the people generally against infanticide rapidly gains strength, and there can be little doubt that, under the fear of the law and the influence of public opinion, the custom which has yet been only checked since annexation, will in a few years cease to exist."*

In the beginning of the following year (on the 2nd January, 1854), the Jhelum (*fabulosus Hydaspes*) witnessed on its banks a joint meeting, arranged by Captain C. Browne of Jhelum, and Mr. Sapte of Goojrat, for these adjacent districts. Here the same plan which had succeeded so well at Goojranwalla and Rawul Pindee was tried, and with the same success; the agreements entered into at Umritsur were presented for consideration, and were "immediately and cordially" adopted. At this meeting, and closely connected with the object of it, was presented a petition signed by the whole assembly, entreating redress from another evil which had grown up under our rule. Adultery had always been regarded by the races of the Punjab with such abhorrence, that nothing short of the death or mutilation of the parties implicated would appease their revenge. Such retribution an injured husband did not scruple to exact under former rule; and he did so with impunity; the law, being too weak to

* Selections from Punjab Correspondence, vol. ii. p. 171.

punish the crime itself, did not attempt to restrain the man who took the punishment into his own hands. Our rule had put a check to this indulgence in unlawful revenge, but had not substituted any penalty for the crime adequate to its enormity in their eyes, or sufficient to deter others from committing it; and therefore immorality among the women had greatly increased. It was for the remedy of this evil that the meeting petitioned, and, as subsequent measures show, not without effect.

At Shahpore, also, on the banks of the Chenab, Mr. Thornton, with Major Hollings, his Deputy Commissioner, held a meeting on the 23rd and 24th January, on which occasion it was ascertained from the heads of the principal Mahomedan and Hindoo families that the practice of female infanticide had not obtained since the commencement of the British rule; that they considered the measures proposed for the suppression of the crime as a proof of kindness and consideration, as well as of the justice of their present rulers, for which they offered their sincere thanks. They affirmed their entire and hearty concurrence in the arrangements proposed for the reduction of the unnecessary expenses hitherto incurred on occasion of betrothal and marriage of their daughters, and their determination to act up to the spirit of the agreements, which they had signed in good faith, and with a full knowledge of the obligations they had voluntarily taken upon themselves.

"I cannot avoid," says Major Hollings, "expressing an earnest hope that the people will not only most faithfully adhere to the agreements in the present instance, but that they will, day by day, more and more feel that the promotion of their real good is the object of the greatest importance to those who rule over them."

In the mean while, the Commissioners of Mooltan and Leia, Mr. Edgeworth and Major Ross, in whose divisions infanticide was not very prevalent, and chiefly confined to Mahomedans of the royal races and some of spurious origin, arranged to hold a joint meeting for their two divisions at Mooltan, a place which will ever be connected in the minds of Englishmen with the melancholy end of Anderson and Agnew, and the treachery of Moolraj. This meeting took place on the 29th December, 1853. The nature of the agreements entered into at Umritsur were explained to them, and were adopted with certain modifications in the rates, &c.

A very important collateral movement was being attempted at this time by Mr. Forsyth, who had succeeded Mr. Bayley as Deputy Commissioner of Kangra, among the high Rajpoots of those Hills. He considered that though the simple principles inaugurated at Umritsur were sufficient to remove the prejudice or pride of comparatively recent date which tempted Bedees, Khutrees, &c., into the crime, yet with the high Rajpoots, where the practice of ages had given a prescriptive force to the inhuman custom, other measures would be necessary to ensure success; though, with the example of the Chohans before us, we can scarcely see this necessity. He also brought to notice the growth of another evil. It has been observed, in connexion with the Jhelum meeting, that our laws, in the moderation which they showed in punishing the crime of adultery, and the strictness with which they forbid the sufferer to take such ruthless retribution, gave some impunity to the adulterer, and encouragement to female immorality. It was believed that they had the same effect in the case of betrothal contracts. Among these Hill Rajpoots there prevailed a custom which it may be interesting to notice, amounting to the systematic sale of daughters. To effect a marriage contract, two families would frequently enter into an agreement that the father of the girl should receive in exchange for his daughter a bride for one of his own family, or else an equivalent in money or goods. So completely was this regarded as a commercial transaction, that, as reported by Mr. Barnes, "in former times, a man dying without heirs, and holding a promised bride, or Natha, as she was called, the Natha was regularly entered in the inventory of his goods." Report tells of "a man who absconded in arrears of revenue, being the holder of a Natha, when the poor child was brought to auction like any other appreciable commodity, and sold to the highest bidder." Under this system, when even unborn daughters become articles of barter and contract, nothing was more frequent than the violation of such contract: to obtain a second bridegroom, and with him a second large sum, for a bride already bought by another man, was an almost daily occurrence.

In the olden time, when any bridegroom elect found himself thus cheated of his betrothed by the faithlessness of her father, nothing was more common than to take the law into his own hands, and, at the head of a body of stalwart comrades, attack the house where the betrothed was concealed, and carry her off in triumph. Law did not, in such cases, interfere to punish the unlawfulness of the act, in tacit acknowledgment of the injustice which gave rise to it. But, under our rule, the only redress for such a breach of agreement was to be looked for through a suit in a civil court, where "damages," the only punishment assignable, would prove "a poor salve to the wounded honor of a jilted bridegroom." Thus, in reality, all check or restraint on such breach of contract was removed. This evil certainly was not fully met by the Umritsur Resolutions.

The plan suggested by Mr. Forsyth for overcoming this double evil was to revive the old Hindoo system of Punchayut. The Punchayut, as has been noticed, is a court or tribunal of native origin, so called from its properly consisting of five (panch) members. Every city and town has its permanent Punchayut, or municipal council, though greatly shorn of power and importance under our rule. Punchayuts of classes or castes are still frequently formed on emergency to decide any abstruse point of Hindoo law.

The proposition was to constitute the Punchayuts local offices of registry and record. Every birth, and even advanced pregnancy, was to be registered; every female infant's life watched, and all marriage contracts supervised and reported by them. On the necessity or expediency of such a system among that single race, in addition to the principles adopted at Umritsur, we do not feel competent to offer an opinion here.

At a later period, Mr. Melvill, the Deputy Commissioner of Umballa, appears to have distinguished himself by his zeal in suppressing a somewhat similar practice among a large body of Rajpoots of inferior rank who abound in the Umballa district. Having held small meetings under the several Tehseeldars, where rates of expenditure were agreed upon, he effected a gathering at Umballa of all the leading men of the different Tehseels, at which he himself presided, and persuaded them to adopt one general scale of expenses, on the Umritsur plan. He also adopted the same plan with the rival clans of Manjha and Malwa Sikhs, and induced them to renounce their wasteful system of marriage expenditure, and, as a most important step towards success, prohibited the customs called Dakhila and Bara among them.*

Mr. Brandreth, too, at Ferozepore, set himself earnestly to suppress this evil among the Doghurs of that neighbourhood. These men appeared to have been the victims of a similar system to that which has been mentioned as prevailing among the Kangra Rajpoots, the rapacity of brides' fathers, who, like the Lahoreens, actually laid an embargo on the marriage of their daughters until their extortionate demands are complied with. With this evil Mr. Brandreth resolved to grapple.

But the most important, as well as most interesting, of these subsidiary meetings, second only to that of Umritsur itself, was one held in the territory of our neighbour, the Maharajah Gholab Singh, King of Cashmere, at a small town called Budheeal, nearly midway between Seealkote and Jummoo. The circumstances which led to this meeting are thus explained by Mr. C. Raikes, under whose auspices it was held. On reaching the station of Seealkote, in the course of his annual cold-

* For accounts of these two parts of the marriage ceremony, see chap. viii.

weather tour, in the beginning of 1854, he "received an invitation from the Prince Runbheer Singh, son and heir apparent of the Maharajah Gholab Singh, to unite with him in calling upon the Rajpoots, and other tribes under the Cashmere hills, to suppress female infanticide, and to regulate marriage expenses."*

Budheeal was selected for this meeting for two reasons: as being the nearest and most accessible town to our frontier, and also as an important "granary," from which the Prince could the more easily exercise Eastern hospitality, by providing for the wants of all his assembled guests and for their various retinues. The whole arrangements were made by Mr. J. Inglis, the Deputy Commissioner of Seealkote, whose cordial co-operation and valuable assistance formed subjects of especial praise in Mr. Raikes's official report of the meeting. The author has hitherto performed, however imperfectly, the part of the mere chronicler; here he claims permission to lay aside that character, and in presenting himself to the reader as an eye-witness, to indulge in the happy reminiscences of that day's proceedings.

Starting from Seealkote at daylight on the 17th of March, 1854, a sharp ride of fourteen miles in the fresh, cool morning air, known only in the Punjab, brought our little party to the scene of action. We passed from the Seealkote military cantonment, with its grand array of officers' bungalows and barracks, crossed its broad line of parade-grounds, and broader plain which spreads

* Had Mr. Raikes been unable to attend this meeting, the Prince had determined to hold one in a more central position for his kingdom, in order to give full force to the Umritsur measures among his Rajpoot subjects.

beyond, until we reached certain boundary pillars in the depth of a jungle, which told us we were no longer on English ground, but had entered the territories of the Jummoo Rajah. Here the scenery seemed to undergo a change: in the place of an open meidan (or plain) we found ourselves threading our way through a low jungle of brushwood, interspersed here and there with topes (or groves) of the Keekur-tree,* and an occasional sacred Peepul,† casting its welcome shade over some humble well and its adjacent cot. As we advanced, the road, or by-path, led us under the walls of villages, along the banks of little streams, whose devious course and uncertain width clearly indicated their original connexion with the mountain torrents from the neighbouring heights, and every step now showed signs of our near approach to the region of the Hills, which towered up in front, on one of the spurs of which could be distinguished, at a probable distance of twelve or fourteen miles, the Maharajah's hereditary fortress of Jummoo, empurpled in the morning sun. At a turn of the road, round a gentle declivity, the town of Budheeal lay before us, and on a corresponding declivity the goodly array of tents which formed the encampment of Mr. C. Raikes and several other civilians and officers who had ridden over the day before. Shortly after, our numbers were still further increased by the arrival of a small party of sportsmen, who had been amusing themselves

* The Keekur, called also Babool, is the Acacia Arabica, or Mimosa Arabica, of science, the tree from which "gum arabic" is extracted.

† The Peepul, or ficus religiosa, is held by the Hindoos in special reverence, and is generally found shading their walls.

at the expense of the bristly denizens of the neighbouring jungle, and were willing to forego saddle and spear for one day to witness this interesting ceremony.

All the preliminaries of the meeting had been arranged on the previous day between Mr. Raikes and the Jummoo Dewan (or chamberlain), a scale of proposed rates prepared, and a scheme of regulations, modified from the Umritsur schedules, submitted for examination; and the manner in which all were drawn up indicated that the greatest care and pains had been bestowed by the Prince and his advisers on the subject, and betokened a sincerity and earnestness, and a far-seeing policy, which reflected honor on all concerned. The usual interchange of courtesy between the Prince and the Commissioner having been gone through in the early part of the day, it was arranged that the Durbar, or meeting, should take place at three o'clock P.M. A little before that hour the heavy dragoons of the Maharajah, in bright glistening helmets and French uniforms, headed by their discordant band, drew up in front of the Commissioner's tent; after them the state elephants, on one of which sat the young Rajah, Motee Singh, nephew to Gholab Singh, the youngest son of Runjeet's old minister, Dheean Singh, who came to represent his uncle and his cousin, and to convey the Commissioner and his friends to the Durbar tent. Then came the "mounting in hot haste:" various were the howdahs, of English and native construction, of every shape, from the cramped-up, double-seated phaeton, with royal arms emblazoned, to that low, flat, tray-like construction which consigns European legs to Asiatic contortions; and, last of all, the least ornamental, but by far the most easy, the simple padding lashed on to the elephant's back with strong ropes. Thus mounted, to our taste, or our opportunity, we set off, some forty in number, to pass from our camp to the Prince's tents on the opposite slope. Here the Commissioner's arrival was announced by a salute of cannon and a vigorous flourish of trumpets, which settled down into "God save the Queen" by the whole band. The Prince then came forward to receive Mr. Raikes, and led him up a long enclosed space to the place of honor in the centre of the Durbar tent, the other civilians and officers being handed in by the different members of the Prince's personal staff. The whole party were arranged in a semicircle, the Prince sitting in the centre, with Mr. Raikes on his right hand and Mr. Inglis on his left, and all the rest distributed themselves towards either side, while the leading men of the Jummoo and Seealkote districts (which here adjoin), the Punches, or municipal corporations, from the small towns, the Lumberdars (landholders) from the villages, &c., &c., were seated on the ground in the centre. The Prince then rose to introduce Mr. Raikes to the meeting, and to solicit him to explain fully all the steps that had been taken by the English within their own territories for the suppression of the crime.

Mr. Raikes then addressed the assembly to the following effect: he commenced by alluding to the evils of marriage expenses, debt, poverty, and disgrace; but chief of all, that crime to which they had given rise, the murder of their daughters. "The Prince and the Maharajah," said he, "have resolved to put this down. They have invited me here to tell you all that we have done at

Mynpooree, and Jullundhur, and Hosheyarpore, and especially under the immediate orders of the Governor-General of India at Umritsur." (Here the several letters and documents connected with these meetings, and the declarations there entered into, were read.) "The object of all this is to induce you, also, to reduce your present foolish marriage expenses. Give to your children and your grandchildren the thousands of rupees that you have hitherto squandered away on your Bhâts and Chârans, who, after they have flattered you, and got your money, turn away and laugh at your folly. Are you afraid of attempting such a change,—at giving up so old and evil a custom? Here," said the Commissioner, "stands Hurree Chund, the Maharajah's confidential and wealthy minister: let us ask him what he thinks of the new plan. 'Hurree Chund, some three years ago you married one of your family; how much did it cost you?' 'Fifteen thousand rupees.' 'A few months ago, since the Umritsur meeting, you married another at Lahore; what did you spend then?' 'One thousand rupees.' Now, my friends, do you go and act on this principle. Where you have hitherto been accustomed to throw away a thousand rupees, now spend a hundred instead; and rest assured your children will be quite as contented, and you yourselves far more happy. But remember, it is not only your money we want to save. I know, as well as you do, that there is another, and far greater evil, arising from this custom; that it tempts you to destroy your female infants to save your purses. This must not be. That crime is forbidden in your own holy books, and will not go unpunished. But why should you ever again commit it?

You see, now, you can save both your money and your daughters' lives. Will you do it? Punches and Zemindars! do you understand what I have said? Do you consent to adopt this reduced scale of payments? Will you, like your brother Rajpoots of Mynpooree and Hosheyarpore, rescue yourselves from this custom, with all its ruinous and inhuman consequences? If so, hold up your right hands in proof of your readiness to sign the agreements which your Prince has drawn up." (At that moment the whole body of the Punches and Zemindars who occupied the centre of the space, with one impulse raised their right hands, and cried, "We will, we will!") "And now, farewell; you have often assembled together in former days to plan for carrying on war, for seizing lands, or even dethroning Rajahs and chiefs. You are assembled to-day for a peaceful purpose, to save the lives of innocent babes, to secure to your homes the welcome presence of daughters. And in this good work may Heaven's blessing rest on you."

This address, so plain and simple, yet so animated and earnest, left a deep impression. Few of that large assembly of simple-minded men could resist the appeal thus touchingly made to their hearts as well as their reason.

The Prince himself then addressed a few words to the meeting, expressive of his cordial approval of the humane measures, and pledging himself for the Maharajah, as an earnest of sincere co-operation, to revoke a *cess*, or tax, of one hundred rupees which had hitherto been levied in the Jummoo territory on all marriages, and to lighten by every means in his power the expenses attendant on the marriages of his subjects. Another very important question was also mooted by the Prince, which may well form matter for future consideration—the propriety of dividing the expense of all marriages between the families of the two contracting parties, by which arrangement the value of a daughter would become equal to that of a son, her life be as precious as his, and the great motive to its destruction be entirely removed. The meeting then ended, and an hospitable entertainment by the Prince, with a display of fireworks, closed the day's proceedings.*

By these subsidiary meetings the results of the great moral demonstration at Umritsur were being diffused throughout the Punjab, and, as Mr. Montgomery rejoiced to report, "a most marked and striking change was becoming perceptible in the social customs of the people." The general success of these meetings was duly notified to the Governor-General, who again repeated how deep a sense the Indian Government entertained of the social importance of this object, and of the value of the exertions which were being so nobly and laudably made.

"The success already achieved," he says, "within the space of a few months, has far exceeded the most sanguine anticipations of the Government, and his Lordship in Council ventures to utter a feeling of humble confidence that a blessing will rest on this good work, whereby it shall be made to spread and prosper.

* To J. Inglis, Esq., the Deputy Commissioner of Seealkote, was due the entire praise for the admirable arrangements of this meeting; and a distinguished officer present (Colonel Graham, then at the head of the Punjab Thuggee department), who had formerly been assistant to the Resident of Delhi, and was accustomed to Indian pageantry, observed, that of the many he had witnessed, he had never seen so imposing a spectacle, nor so well regulated a Durbar.

"His Lordship in Council requests that you will convey the sincere and cordial thanks of the Government to Mr. Montgomery, the Judicial Commissioner, as well as to the Commissioners, Mr. Raikes, Mr. Thornton, Mr. Edgworth, and Major Ross, to the Deputy Commissioners, Mr. Inglis, Mr. Carnac, Captain Browne, and Major Clarke, and to all who have been mentioned with commendation in these reports.

"Especially the Governor-General in Council would desire to congratulate Mr. Raikes on the special success of the meeting held near Seealkote, which gave gratifying proof that the example set by the British Government had been applauded and followed by the foreign state upon our borders.

"Meean Runbheer Singh fully deserves all the praise which Mr. Raikes has bestowed on him."*

Nor was it enough for Lord Dalhousie to express thus in language, though official, unusual, earnest, and cordial, the approval of the Government of which he was the head. He considered the occasion one on which he might add to that more formal recognition of the services of a valued public servant, the private expression of sympathising approval. He at the same time wrote privately to Mr. Raikes, offering congratulations (to use his own words) "on the spreading success of measures which you were the first to mould, and on the influence they are already exercising over other rules as well

* Extract from letter No. 2259, from G. T. Edmonstone, Esq., Secretary to the Government of India, to John Lawrence, Esq., Chief Commissioner of the Punjab, dated Fort William, May 25, 1854.

as our own. There is genuine pleasure in such a sight."*

* The author has experienced no ordinary gratification in being permitted to insert this valuable letter entire:

"Government House,
March 27, 1854.

"MY DEAR SIR,—Mr. Courtenay has just shown me your letter of the 19th inst. and its enclosure. Without expending a sentence in assuring you of the full and cordial approbation with which I have learned your meeting with Meer Runbheer Singh, I beg to congratulate you on the spreading success of the measures which you were the first to mould, and on the influence they are already exercising over other rules as well as our own. There is genuine pleasure in such a sight. I will most readily act on your suggestions regarding the Meer whenever the official letter reaches me.

"I beg to remain,
"Very faithfully yours,
"DALHOUSIE.

"Charles Raikes, Esq."

What a striking contrast does the earnest, warm-hearted tone of the foregoing extracts, which the formalities of official language cannot altogether conceal, afford to the cold, measured terms in which the proposal made just fifty years ago by Jonathan Duncan, to attempt the suppression of this crime, was received by the Supreme Government of India, as expressed in a letter addressed to him on the 31st of July, 1806:

"We cannot but contemplate with approbation the considerations of humanity which have induced you to combine, with the proposed expedition, the project of suppressing the barbarous custom of female infanticide. But the speculative success, even of that benevolent project, cannot be considered to justify the prosecution of measures which may expose to hazard the essential interests of the State; although, as a collateral object, the pursuit of it would be worthy of the benevolence and humanity of the British Government."—Given in Moor's Hindoo Infanticide, p. 37.

CHAPTER XII.

STATISTICS OF FEMALE INFANTICIDE.

Statistics—Those of 1852 and subsequent years compared, showing that the crime did greatly prevail, and is rapidly decreasing—Census of the Kangra Rajpoots analysed—Of Munhâs clans of Seealkote district—Great reduction in marriage expenditure effected—Mr. Raikes's letter of approval to five hundred and thirty-seven families—His forbidding claims on breach of marriage contracts to exceed the Umritsur stipulations—The census of the Bedees of Derah Baba Nanuk—The Chief Commissioner's visit in 1855—Improvement also among those in the Gogaira district—Mr. Campbell's remarks on infanticide considered.

It may, perhaps, be objected that the justice of the charge of infanticide, as brought against these Punjab races, has hitherto been rather assumed than proved; that no statistical evidence has been brought forward to show that, after all, this unnatural custom really has obtained among them to so great an extent. The omission of such proof was designed. It would have been very easy, had it been necessary, to produce statistical data which would have left the prevalence of this terrible crime beyond all doubt,—unless, indeed, some ingenious theory could be suggested, by which the glaring disproportion of sexes, and the confessions of all classes, might be otherwise satisfactorily explained and accounted for. But our desire was to avoid needlessly burdening our pages with elaborate statistical tables, which have but little attraction for the general reader, especially as it was intended to bring forward, at a later stage of the investigation, some of the very valuable information of this nature placed at our disposal, which might thus answer the double purpose of confirming the truth of the charge, and proving the reality of the success which had attended the measures adopted for suppressing the crime, by contrasting the more recent returns with those previously made. We now proceed to carry out this part of our plan. It is necessary, however, to premise that the statistical information which was obtained during the years 1852-53, and prior to that date, though, doubtless, generally speaking, correct, cannot be so closely relied on as that of later date. There was less uniformity of system, and less accuracy, in collecting; moreover, feelings of pride or mistrust on the part of parents and heads of families may have induced them to withhold domestic particulars, or to give inaccurate information, which at that time there was no means of checking and correcting. Still, on the whole, the returns made in the first years after annexation were sufficiently correct to convey a tolerably clear idea of the population of any particular district, though the want of a uniform system rendered it less safe for purposes of collation and comparison.

From Kangra, the home of the high Rajpoots of the Punjab, most interesting statistics have been obtained for the year 1852, through Mr. E. C. Bayley (who was then Deputy Commissioner of that district). The following table, prepared from information collected by him, will give a condensed view of the proportions of the male and female population at that time.

It may be noticed that in this, and all the following Kangra returns, those from the Kooloo Tehseel are not included. These have been intentionally omitted; for that district contains very few Rajpoots—only twenty-four families out of a population of above 26,000 Hindoos—and, with the single exception of the Rajah's house, is believed to be free from this crime. Indeed, the very atmosphere of Kooloo seems inimical to Rajpoot purity and pride, and to infanticide; even a Kutoch, or Golehria, or Juswal, who takes up his residence in Kooloo, becomes an outcast, and is at once regarded by his blood relations as a Kenait, with whom intermarriage is no longer possible. Thus with the loss of social position disappears among them this motive to infanticide.

CENSUS of four of the five Tehseels of the Kangra District, as collected by E. C. Bayley, Esq., Deputy Commissioner, for the year 1852.

Name of Tehseel.	Hindoos of all Classes.				
	Adults.		Children under five.		Per-centage of girls to boys.
	Men.	Women.	Boys.	Girls.	
Kangra	53,508	45,321	26,266	22,667	86·29
Nadown	75,644	61,580	32,444	26,402	81·37
Noorpoor	43,995	33,439	21,346	16,103	75·43
Hurreepoor	33,305	24,395	12,721	12,646	99·41
Total	206,452	164,735	92,777	77,818	83·87

Name of Tehseel.	Rajpoots of all Grades.				
	Adults.		Children under five.		Per-centage of girls to boys.
	Men.	Women.	Boys.	Girls.	
Kangra	3,334	3,049	1,700	995	58·52
Nadown	6,294	5,999	2,901	2,307	79·52
Noorpoor	3,975	3,284	1,444	1,103	76·38
Hurreepoor	6,575	4,530	2,461	2,337	94·96
Total	20,178	16,832	8,506	6,742	79·26

Thus it appears that in the whole Hindoo population of that district, there were about 84 girls to every 100 boys, and even among the whole body of Rajpoots of all grades, the population was nearly 80 girls (varying, however, in different districts from 95 to 58) to every 100 boys.

But, from the same source, a more detailed table of the population of the three highest Rajpoot clans of that district will show that, while in the Rajpoot body the disproportion was scarcely less than among the whole Hindoo population (including, be it remembered, Bedees, Sodhees, Lahoreens, &c., &c.), an examination of the statistics of their different clans discovers so vast a disparity among the higher ones, as to prove that among them the crime had been frightfully prevalent.

Name of Tribes.	Adults.		Children.		Per-centage of girls to boys.
	Men.	Women.	Boys.	Girls.	
Kutoch	832	612	382	154	40·31
Pathanea	2500	2000	1044	350	33·52
Golehrias	1501	800	574	125	21·75
Total	4833	3412	1900	629	33·10

By this it will be seen how greatly the disproportion increases among the higher clans; that the per-centage of 79 among the whole Rajpoots dwindles down to 21·75 among the Golehrias, or little more than 20 unmarried girls to every 100 boys under five years of age.

Such were the statistical discoveries made by Mr. Bayley among the Kangra Rajpoots in 1852—discoveries which cried aloud for redress.

The measures adopted for the remedy of this evil have been already noticed. The result of them, up to the present time, may be gathered from the following calculation, giving a census of the children of various ages who were alive in 1855 in the Kangra district, and belonging to families known to have formerly practised infanticide :

STATEMENT showing Census of Children in the Villages practising Infanticide for the year 1855.

Name of Tehseel.	From four to fourteen years of age.		Of four years of age.		Of three years of age.		Of two years of age.		Of one year of age and under.		Total.	
	Male.	Female.	Male.	Female.	Male.	Female.	Male.	Female.	Male.	Female.	Male.	Female.
Kangra	514	245	67	50	47	41	76	47	81	74	785	457
Nadown......	1171	515	194	148	195	183	218	147	235	204	2013	1197
Noorpoor	697	203	146	72	141	62	146	53	184	99	1314	489
Hurreepoor..	760	269	122	65	91	87	142	93	176	111	1291	625
Total	3142	1233	529	335	474	373	582	340	676	488	5403	2768

A glance at these tables will show the rapid progress which has been made towards the preservation of female life, even among these proud Rajpoots of Kangra. Of all the children born and preserved during the last four years, the girls numbered 1536, and the boys 2261; whereas, of those preserved during the whole of the preceding ten years, the girls had only amounted to 1233, while the boys were 3142. Of these between four and fourteen years of age, the girls bore the proportion to the boys of less than 40 per cent., forming scarcely one-fourth of the whole juvenile Rajpoot population of the district; whereas, of those under four years old, the proportion had reached 67 girls to every 100 boys.

The following table, however, as based on the foregoing calculation, will more clearly show the comparative increase:

Name of Tehseel.	Total number of children under fourteen years.			Children from four to fourteen years of age.			Children of four years and under.		
	Boys.	Girls.	Percentage of boys to girls.	Boys.	Girls.	Percentage of girls to boys.	Boys.	Girls.	Percentage of girls to boys.
Kangra	785	457	58·21	514	245	47·66	271	212	78·22
Nadown	2013	1197	54·46	1171	515	43·93	842	682	80·99
Noorpoor	1314	489	37·21	697	203	29·12	617	286	46·35
Hurreepoor	1291	625	48·41	760	269	35·39	531	356	67·04
Total	5403	2768	51·25	3142	1232	39·21	2261	1536	67·93

This improvement, it must be remembered, has taken place entirely among the higher classes, where, as has been already shown, the disproportion of the sexes was most appalling, proving too clearly that the crime was most prevalent among them.

This decreasing inequality between the sexes shows (to use the words of Mr. R. P. Jenkins, the Deputy Commissioner of the district, to whom the author is indebted for these later returns) that "the crime is wonderfully checked." "In my last tour through the district," he says, "I learnt that many, very many, families now owned daughters who formerly were never known to possess any."

Passing on to that other class of Rajpoots called Munhâses, who reside on the low lands along the foot of the

Himalayas from the Ravee to the Jhelum, the following most valuable and interesting statistical table will show how deeply that class had been imbued with this infanticidal spirit, and how English rule has operated to rescue their helpless babes from destruction.

In fifty Rajpoot villages in the Seealkote district a careful analysis of the population produced the following result :*

Boys.	Girls.					
	Above eight years old.	Between eight and six years old.	Between six and three years old.	Three years and under.	Total.	
462	5	16	40	129	190	Munhâs Rajpoots.

Thus of all female children born in these villages prior to 1846, there remained alive only 5 in 1854; but of those born in the years 1846 and 1847—the period of our first intercourse with the Sikh Durbar—16 were preserved, with a progressive increase during succeeding years, until, in the eight years between 1846 and 1853 inclusive, the number amounted to 190.

But still a more exact view of this increase may be obtained by the annexed table, which includes the children of the whole Munhâs population of the Seeälkote district, and gives the yearly proportions, whereas in the preceding one only fifty villages in which the Munhâs preponderated were taken, and the numbers given for two and three years together.

* For the particulars given in this table, the author begs to acknowledge his obligation to E. Prinsep, Esq., settlement officer of the district.

ABSTRACT Statement of the children of the Munhâs tribe in the District of Seealkote, born and preserved between the years 1850 and 1854.

Between four and five years old. Born in 1850.	Between three and four years old. Born in 1851.	Between two and three years old. Born in 1852.	Between two and one year old. Born in 1853.	One year and under. Born in 1854.	Total of five years of age and under.
15	23	39	53	96	226

The most remarkable fact here shown is, that, in the year 1854, there were preserved above six times as many female infants as there had been in 1850.

Nor must we omit to mention here—what gives the strongest security for a permanence of this improvement—that the principle of reducing marriage expenditure has been openly and very extensively carried out by this class, as the following table will show:*

STATEMENT of the number and expense of marriages in the Seealkote District during the years 1854 and 1855, in which the parties acted up to the engagements entered into by them at Umritsur and Budheeal.

Year.	Number of marriages in which reduction was made.	Amount now spent.	Amonnt spent by the same parties on former occasions.
		r. a. p.	r. a. p.
1854	537	19,086 10 0	49,061 8 0
1855	2325	38,996 4 0	85,062 8 0

Thus showing that, in the 537 families in which marriages were contracted during 1854 on these economical principles, there were spent only 19,086 rupees, or on an

* This table was prepared by Mr. Inglis on the following plan: at every marriage occurring in his district, the Putwarree, or registrar of the town or village, inquired of the bride's father what expense they had incurred, and also what they had spent on the occasion of the last marriage in the family, and these statements were generally confirmed by the testimony of disinterested neighbours; and from the information thus obtained the above table was compiled.

average of 35 rupees on each marriage; whereas in the very same families the sum of 49,061 rupees had been expended on the same number on former occasions, giving an average of about 91 rupees on each, thereby effecting a saving of above 30,000 rupees, or a reduction of nearly two-thirds of the former expenditure. This cheering fact, when duly reported to Mr. Raikes, elicited from that officer a letter of approval,* addressed to every one of the 537 heads of families who had so acted. The result was, as will be seen by the above table, a still more general adoption of the principle during the year 1855 by 2325 families, at a saving of nearly 50,000 rupees, and giving an average of about 16 rupees on each marriage.

While Mr. Raikes was thus enabled to encourage those parents who exercised economy under shelter of the Umritsur agreement, he was also called on to exercise his authority to check a returning tendency to extravagance in other quarters in defiance of that agreement. He observed that in some suits for breach of marriage contracts brought to him under appeal, the sums claimed by plaintiffs, on account of expenses incurred at betrothals, had been fixed extravagantly high. He thereupon addressed a letter throughout his division, requesting that officers, when called on to decide on any such suits, should bear in mind that the rates agreed upon at the Umritsur meeting should form their guide in awarding damages.† Thus the terms of their own agreements, and the scale of expenses voluntarily adopted by them-

* See Appendix.

† Circular letter, No. 333, of 1855, from Commissioner to Deputy Commissioners of the Lahore Division.

selves, under the sanction of Government, received the force of a law to which, as being self-imposed, they could with the less justice object.

The same happy results are discovered among the Bedees, too, who were the most notorious for the systematic perpetration of this crime.

Major Herbert Edwardes, in his able Report on the subject, already so often cited, says that, from a census carefully taken in the beginning of the year 1852, it was found that, among this class, consisting of some 300 families in the Jullundhur district, only two daughters had been preserved under the Sikh rule, whereas at that time there were living among them nearly fifty daughters under four years of age. But the following very valuable statistical table, prepared by Mr. Maddocks, who was lately the Deputy Commissioner of that district, gives a more detailed statement of this increase:

ABSTRACT of Births and Deaths of Bedee children, male and female, from 1847-48, to December, 1854.

Year.	Number of boys and girls born.		Number of boys and girls died.		Alive.	
	Boys.	Girls.	Boys.	Girls.	Boys.	Girls.
1847-48*	27	12	13	4	14	8
1848-49	37	17	9	7	28	10
1849-50	37	14	13	8	24	6
1850-51	33	21	13	9	20	12
1851-52	18	18	8	7	10	11
1852-53	22	16	7	7	15	9
1853-54	27	19	10	5	17	14
1854-55	20	33	3	5	17	28
Total	221	150	76	52	145	98

* The official year of the Indian Government runs from April 1st to March 31st. It should be marked that in all these tables this calculation is retained, though the number of the first year only is given.

In January, 1855, Mr. Lawrence, the Chief Commissioner, visited Derah Bab Nanuk, the head-quarters of this race, when Mr. Raikes, in connexion with Mr. Maddocks, had the gratification to present to him some 80 infant Bedee girls, of whom as many as 28 had been born in the preceding twelve months. These little girls, led by their fathers, who did not fear to own that they had violated the unnatural order of their race, and apparently proud and fond of their offspring, which a few years before they would have been ashamed or afraid to own, attested in the strongest and most convincing manner to the reality of the success which had followed on the measures instituted in the Punjab for the abolition of this crime. To Mr. Lawrence, who, as we have seen, had ever evinced so deep an interest in this movement, the sight of these living witnesses to the humane and Christian spirit of the Government could have been scarcely less gratifying than to Mr. Raikes himself, who beheld in them such cheering assurance that years of thought and labor devoted to this holy cause had not been spent in vain.

The latest accounts of the progress of this reform we quote from Mr. Raikes's last Annual Report. "There are now," he says, "200 Bedee girls to 400 boys of seven years and under." The same improvement is perceptible among the Bedees in the Gogaira district. There were, in 1851, 30 boys and only 3 girls, 2 of whom were daughters of Sumpoorun Singh, who was mentioned in a former chapter as having preserved 1 at the request of Lord Hardinge in 1846. There are now, in 1856, 11 boys and 6 girls under five years of age.

The foregoing statistics refer only to the three classes in the Punjab who were most notorious for the perpetration of this crime—the Rajpoots of the Kangra and Jummoo groups, the Munhâses, and the Bedees. It is unnecessary to add any particulars regarding the other races involved in the same charge. These will, it is hoped, suffice to prove to the unprejudiced reader that the crime really did exist, and is now rapidly decreasing, and almost extinct.

We are aware that a writer of some power and popularity has thought fit to cast a doubt on the existence of the crime altogether in our provinces, and a passing sneer on those whose energies have been so nobly devoted to its suppression. The passage referred to is as follows:

"Child-murder, as it involves concealment of the fact, would not be shown by the reports; and the murder of female infants, at one time common among certain tribes in certain parts of the country, is sometimes represented to be very general in our provinces. But I must say that I doubt the fact. I do not think that it is likely to occur in present prosperous circumstances among large clans, in which there is plenty of room for intermarriages without infringing the rule which prohibits the marriage of blood-relations. In fact, except among isolated families claiming peculiar rank, girls are very valuable. And if child-murder did take place to a great extent, many instances must come to light. If ten such cases be ascertained by the magistrate, we may well believe that ninety are concealed; but if none are found out, I should believe in neither ninety nor nine. I have had to do with a considerable Rajpoot population, and have seen nothing of the kind. I am, therefore, slow to believe speculative people who go into a village, pencil in hand, and, because they fancy that they see more boys than girls, calculate and propound that exactly one-half of the female infants of the ordinary agricultural Rajpoots are annually murdered."*

Now, we are tempted to hope that the reader of the foregoing pages will not be unwilling to give credence to the tale, sad though it be, of the systematic destruction of female infants in India. He will, we think, see proof indisputable of the prevalence of this crime, both in the former disparity, and also in the now increasing equality of the sexes; let us add a hope, too, that, with us, he will not be disposed to place in the category of "speculative people who go about, pencil in hand," and give play to their fancy, in support of a crotchet at the expense of sober reason and sound judgment, such men as Jonathan Duncan, Alexander Walker, J. P. Willoughby, Launcelot Wilkinson, James Thomason, Robert Montgomery, and Charles Raikes.

* Campbell's Modern India and its Government, p. 500. In justice to Mr. Campbell, it should be mentioned that at the time he wrote the above the anti-infanticidal movement had not extended to the Punjab. It is possible that his recent experience among these races may induce him to qualify his opinion.

CHAPTER XIII.

CONCLUDING REMARKS.

The present system on sounder principles, and more likely to be of permanent effect—It enlists the natural feelings and the mother's influence—Further steps necessary, especially among the Kangra Rajpoots, to induce marriages on equal terms—A second general meeting desirable—Arrangements for marrying daughters now preserved—The system should be extended over India—Its secondary motives not to be despised—May pave the way for Christianity—Remarriage of widows to be considered—Its present prohibition inconsistent, fraught with evil—Steps now being taken by Hindoo community and by Government for its removal—Probable results—Conclusion.

"WILL this crime, after all, be completely suppressed?" We do not hesitate to avow our conviction that it will. "If other attempts have failed, if the earlier measures, which at the outset gave good promise of success, disappointed men's expectations, it may be asked, what is there to lead to the belief that the present system will be more efficacious?" To this we can only answer, that, without for one moment attempting to depreciate or disparage the exertions of those earnest men whose names are so nobly connected with the earlier history of this movement, we still cannot refrain from expressing our opinion, that the plans introduced by Duncan and Walker, and the men who followed in their steps, had not in them the elements of permanent success.* True, the whole weight of civil authority, supported by immense personal influence, might be, and was, brought to bear upon the evil; but no sooner was the force of that authority relaxed, or that personal influence removed, than the crime began again to rear its hydra form. From a merely coercive system, with its "covenants," reluctantly signed and nugatory, supported by espionage and fine, still more reluctantly and sullenly acceded to, and virtually inoperative, little of permanent good was to be looked for. It tended to drive the proud Rajpoot into a defiant resistance, instead of leading him on to cordial co-operation. Some other motive than a fear of "the powers that be" was needed to give efficiency and permanency to any system for the suppression of this crime; and on this it is that we build our hopes of success from the more recently introduced system of self-legislation, supported and directed by Government, as was first exhibited at Mynpooree, and subsequently expanded at Umritsur. Here the motives for the destruction of daughters, originating partly in pride and partly in the exorbitant marriage expenditure, are being removed, and counter-motives imparted, and an interest created in their preservation, for their own sakes.

* The author is pleased to find that he does not stand alone in the view he has taken of the earlier measures against infanticide; a similar opinion is given by Mr. Kaye, and is thus happily expressed: "Though Duncan and Walker deserved success, it was not in their power to command it. They were the pioneers of humanity and civilisation in that direction, and bravely they labored with axe and hatchet to clear away the dense jungle of barbarism that lay before them; but they did not apply the fire to the root, and the noxious wilderness soon sprung up again above the delusive clearings they had made."—See Kaye's Administration of the East India Company, p. 558.

For the daughter's life, we believe, a lasting guarantee is obtained in the returning freedom of the mother's love, no longer fettered and trampled on by the father's pride. Of the few instances in which mercy has triumphed, has it not been the mother's appeal for that mercy which saved her child? There is the well-known anecdote given by Captain Hall, of the Mairwarrah mother whose entreaty "for Crishna's sake" rescued her babe from death. An instance is given by Mr. Gubbins, where, in the happy absence of her mother from her husband's roof at the time of her child's birth, a little girl was spared. And, though the instances are, indeed, most rare where it can be hoped that such maternal influence has prevailed, yet we may be assured that the mother is rarely a willing, or even a passive participator in the crime: laments and prayers for the life of a doomed infant, though unavailing, have not unfrequently passed beyond the precincts of the closed Zenana.* Everything tends to prove that human nature has not become so utterly degraded; that the Hindoo mother still retains that natural affection, so proverbial as to have received the testimony of inspiration, "Can a mother forget her suckling child?" that in her we have a powerful ally, if only she be allowed the exercise of her influence on the side of mercy; and that even the father, if he can but shake off the trammels of pride and

* "One man, in presence of many others, told me that he remembers his mother's cries when, at the birth of a daughter, she implored her husband to spare her child, her flesh and blood; but monster custom was heedless of the yearning of a fond parent, and the child was consigned alive to a tomb. These unfortunate children were always buried alive."—Extract from a private letter.

custom, will become a no less willing champion of his daughter's life.

Yet let us not be tempted to think nothing more is necessary for the attainment of this permanent success; be it borne in mind that the good is only begun; the principle is not yet so firmly established that it may be left to work out its own results. Parents of all classes are, indeed, rejoicing in the opportunity of preserving their daughters; but there will be found here and there instances where vestiges of former pride and prescriptive custom are still clung to with cruel tenacity, and the resistance of the one or two malcontents in a district may, unless checked, succeed in drawing back again into the vortex of crime hundreds of others who are now struggling to escape beyond its influence.

There is another evil, too, which is beginning to present itself, and which must be promptly guarded against. For the hundreds of girls under five years of age (born and preserved since the annexation of the Punjab), husbands must be provided in a year or two; for the Hindoo father who has been persuaded to spare the life of his child has not yet learned to regard with complacency the possibility of her remaining unmarried. If he shall find that for his daughter, now preserved, he can contract no fitting alliance, her preservation will have been in vain; for her very presence in his family unmarried, will act as a perpetual rebuke and warning to drive him back again into the perpetration of the crime as the only mode of averting the threatened dishonor of his house. Against this evil, which is daily assuming a more formidable aspect, timely measures must be adopted, or the philanthropy of the leaders of this movement will assuredly sustain a bitter reverse. There is more fear for the proud Kangra Rajpoots than for any other class. The Bedees have, it appears, quietly yielded; beneath the decline of their sacerdotal influence—the priesthood of a fast-expiring race—their claims to especial honor and reverence are sinking with the glories of their effete reign; and they have, not unreluctantly, consented to place themselves on a footing with the other Khutree clans. With them, as forming so small a fraction of the Khutree race, the difficulty of arranging becoming marriages for their daughters is inconsiderable; numerically so few, they will, without difficulty, find husbands among the legion of Khutree boys. So, also, with the Sodhees: nor is there any reason to fear for the Lahoreens. It is to the proud princely house of the Kutoch of Kangra that attention must be directed, and to some extent, also, to the Munhâs clans of the plains. So long as these races so jealously retain their distinctions of rank, and with them the old prejudice of marrying a daughter into a higher house, the danger will exist, which their isolated position along this mountain range increases. If only they could be brought, like the Bedees and Khutrees at the Jullundhur meeting, to consent to marriage on equal terms, to give and take daughters among themselves, the danger would disappear, and the only serious obstacle to the entire suppression of infanticide among them would cease. It becomes a subject of grave importance how this evil may be forestalled.

It was generally considered that the Umritsur meeting

of 1853 was only the commencement, the first blow struck at infanticide in the Punjab, to be vigorously followed up at a short interval by another of a similar character. Is not the time now coming for a further demonstration? Would it not be expedient, before the expiration of another year, to invite all those who formed the great conclave of 1853 to assemble again, in order to convey to them the public acknowledgments of Government for their faithful observance of the agreements then entered into, to give them an opportunity of proclaiming anew their hearty approval of the beneficial measures then adopted, and to produce, if they thought fit, those evidences of their sincerity, the daughters whose lives had been spared? Then the further discussion of the question, the next step in the great national reform, might be taken; and, with sympathies thus enlisted afresh, even these Rajpoots might be induced to throw down the yet remaining barrier which their pride has raised, and consent to seek alliance on equal terms, thus escaping the only difficulty that presents itself to the marriage of the daughters they have preserved.

Nor is the Punjab the only field whereon this difficulty will present itself. To insure the permanency of this system it should be universal. The North-West Provinces still present clans of Rajpoots who have to be won over into the holy league. Rajpootana is not yet pure of the blood of infants. In Oude they have been perishing by thousands, unheeded, in the general maladministration. If only this system of self-legislation assumed the national character it would so easily admit of, instead of being confined to a few clans, or to a province, success would be complete: each tribe, secure in the possession of daughters, and in the means of marrying them honorably, would stimulate its neighbour, and thus a network of interests would cover the Rajpoot race.*

The reader is, perhaps, disposed to think that too much consideration is here shown to the false pride of an idolatrous race; that their prejudices are being handled with too delicate a touch; that such secondary motives and earthly aims are unworthy of the advocacy of one who avows his ministerial character, and who has throughout the foregoing pages sought to take a religious view of this social question. Perhaps so; still he would urge that, until it shall please God in his own good time to permit the successful infusion of the higher and holier influence of Christianity, we should not think lightly of a system which, without openly opposing the Hindoo's hereditary code of honor, counteracts its chief evil, and enables him to enjoy intact any legitimate pride of ancestral descent, and preserve the vaunted purity of his race, without leaving the shadow of a pretext for the commission of so unnatural a crime as infanticide.

Nay, more; may not these very measures pave the way in the end for Christianity itself? May not these efforts, prompted by the pure disinterested benevolence of his Christian rulers, lead the Hindoo to recognise the presence of a higher spirit of morality, to which he is wholly a stranger, and tempt him onward to an examina-

* In the North-West Provinces special commissioners have been already appointed to investigate this subject; but the author is not able to add to the foregoing history any of the results of their labors, having been unsuccessful in his endeavours to obtain the necessary information.

tion into its origin and character, until he be led to embrace the purer faith of the Gospel?

In connexion with the position of the female sex, another remarkable feature of the Hindoo system requires to be noticed.

The Hindoo, as has been stated, entirely disbelieves in the existence of female virtue; in his opinion, celibacy and chastity are incompatible; to remain unmarried is with him to become dishonored. Yet, paradoxical though it may seem, that very system which, as a safeguard of virtue, enjoins marriage at the earliest stage of puberty, forbids the child once betrothed, even if her affianced die before she be old enough to contract marriage, to be betrothed a second time, dooms her young life to compulsory, hopeless widowhood; thus throwing her into the very furnace of temptation, from which he considers it impossible she can escape unscathed. The Hindoo, therefore, who, acting out this false system of morality, in his jealousy of female honor, is tempted to sacrifice the new-born daughter rather than risk the danger of an unmarried life, does not scruple, with glaring inconsistency, by the very prohibition of a second marriage, to drive the widowed child, as the victim of temptation or want, to swell the ranks of Nach girls and prostitutes.

The existence of this crying evil has been long felt by the Hindoos themselves; from the days of Akbar* to the present time, there has ever been a feeling—a strong

* See chap. viii.; the feud of the Lahoreens and Sureens is reported to have originated in this question.

feeling—among an important section of them in favor of its abrogation; but there were found to be far too deeply rooted those promptings of marital jealousy, of which this custom is one, and suttee another (though a most exaggerated) result, to admit of this social reform being generally successful without a great struggle. Brahmanical influence, which could not deduce a shadow of excuse from the dogmas of their Vedas and Shastras for infanticide, will be exerted to the utmost against so startling an innovation as the second marriage of widows; and its introduction must, therefore, be a work of time. Greatly as all must desire to see the annihilation of a custom so fraught with evil, it must be borne in mind that anything like compulsory measures will inevitably retard its accomplishment. From the Hindoos alone, by a spontaneous co-operation among themselves, the effort must come, to be successful. Such a movement has indeed begun already. The Hindoo community have represented their anxiety to shake off the trammels of this revolting custom, and Government has shown itself prepared, and only too ready, to remove all legal obstacles to such a course, and to give the fullest weight of their authority to any prudent acts of self-legislation that may be adopted.*

Then will be gained another and most important step in the restoration of the female Hindoo to her proper position; and the prospect need be no distant one of the child whose frail life has been saved from the grave to

* There is even now, while we are writing, a bill before a select committee of the Legislative Council, the substance of which will be found in the Appendix.

which an unnatural parental pride would have consigned her, and who in maturer years holds her fitting position in her husband's house, becoming herself the mother of children, among whom the hitherto despised daughter may enjoy an equal share of care and love with the more favored son.

There is yet one step further. Much—very much—is now being written and said about the great changes to be effected in the Hindoo character by education. That the infusion of English ideas and English modes of thought will greatly tend to expand the native mind, cannot be doubted; but let it ever be made instrumental in furthering that which should form the ulterior aim of every benevolent design for ameliorating the condition of man—his advancement in true knowledge, and in holiness. Let the principles and precepts of the Gospel sanctify the education of the Hindoo, and then, among other countless blessings which will result from such a system of education, he will learn to recognise the true position of his wife as being an heir, together with him, of the grace of life.*

To the mind of the historian the annals of India present little more than a chronicle of commerce and conquest, where Christianity has no place. The eye of the

* It may be thought that the author has passed over, without due notice, the efforts which are being made throughout India for the promotion of education. It is a subject which he has purposely abstained from dwelling upon, feeling himself at present incompetent to offer any opinion on the merits of the many rival plans for educating the natives which are being propounded. That education should be carried generally into the cities and villages of India he most readily admits, as its tendency, if properly regulated, will certainly be to elevate the tone of morality, as well as to expand the intellect. But he freely admits that it is to mission schools, where alone Christianity is tolerated, as under the Divine blessing the nurseries of the future native Church in India, that he looks with the liveliest interest.

English statesman is turned to her princely revenues and vast patronage, but it is too often closed to the attendant spiritual responsibilities. The Indian chaplain, however, may be permitted to take a somewhat different, though, perhaps, much more narrow-minded, view of the country which is his allotted field of labor; and to confess to a joyous feeling as he traces out, what historian and statesman may little regard, those humbler scenes where "mercy and peace have met together" on this lately troubled land, and to the cheering hope that ere long the remainder of the Psalmist's bright picture may be realised, that in these regions where Heathenism still reigns "Truth may flourish out of the earth, and righteousness look down from Heaven."

SUPPLEMENTAL CHAPTER.

INFANTICIDE AMONG THE ABORIGINES.

Aboriginal races—Gickers of the time of Mahmoud Ghori almost extinct—Khonds of Orissa—Captain Macpherson's successful measures.

It at one time formed part of the plan of this work that one chapter should be devoted to the consideration of the crime of infanticide as perpetrated by the aborigines of India; but much difficulty was experienced in obtaining any satisfactory information on this head: the author's remoteness from the tracts of country occupied by any of these races, and the want of access to books which might throw light upon their religious tenets or social customs, has induced him to forego for the present this portion of his plan, and to content himself with adding, in a supplemental form, a few remarks on the infanticidal tendencies of the only aboriginal race (excepting the Mairs) respecting whom he has been enabled to collect any authentic information.*

* The following particulars respecting the Khonds have been obtained entirely from No. 5 of the Selections from the Records of the Government of India, containing a history of the suppression of human sacrifice and female infanticide in the Hill tracts of Orissa; and also from a highly valuable little work, entitled An Account of the Religion of the Khonds in Orissa, by Captain S. Chartres Macpherson, of the Madras Army.

It should be premised, that although the Mahomedans and Hindoos are always spoken of as the inhabitants of India, neither the one nor the other are indigenous to the country, any more than the Saxons and the Normans were the aborigines of Britain. There were to be found among the jungle fastnesses, especially along those vast mountain ranges generally known as the Eastern and Western Ghâts, and along the Vindhya chain which connects their northern extremities, and also in other parts of India, remains of the barbarous races who originally peopled the country; such as the Todahs of the Neilgherries, the Koles, Khonds, and Sonthals of Orissa and Bengal, the Mairs and Bheels of Rajpootana, and various other races, who have only partially succumbed to the rule or the faith of their conquering invaders.

To what extent these different tribes are involved in the general charge of infanticide we have been unable to discover. So far as we can learn, there are only two races* among whom the crime has been traced to its origin and been perseveringly and successfully suppressed—the Mairs, under the energetic philanthropy of Captain Hall, as already noticed; † and the Khonds, among whom the labors of Captain Macpherson appear to have been attended with great success.

* There is one tribe, however,—now almost lost among the various races that have successively poured in upon India through the great northern gate, the Khyber Pass, and have settled themselves along the mountains and rivers of the Punjab,—known of old by the name of the Gickers, or Ghukkers, a race of wild barbarians, respecting whom a tradition has been preserved, which, if true, confirms the assertion of Ferishtah, the historian, that "they were without either religion or morality." It is reported that "it was a custom among them, as soon as a female child was born, to carry her to the market-place, and there proclaim aloud, holding the child in one hand and a knife in the other, that any person who wanted a wife might now take her, otherwise she was immediately put to death."—Dow's History of Hindostan, vol. i. p. 138.

† See chap. iv.

The Khonds are a numerous and widely-scattered race, occupying the confines, or "border marches," of the Bengal and Madras Presidencies, extending, more or less, from the shores of the Bay of Bengal to the kingdom of Nagpore, and from Cuttack to the Vizagapatam district. They are divided into two great classes, or sects—the "Boora" Khonds and the "Tari" Khonds, or, respectively, the worshippers of Boora Pennu (the God of Light), and of Tari Pennu (the Earth Goddess). The legendary origin of this division is thus given by Captain Macpherson:

"Boora Pennu, in the beginning, created for himself a consort, who became Tari Pennu, or the Earth Goddess, and the source of evil. He afterwards created the earth. As Boora Pennu walked upon it with Tari, he found her wanting in affectionate compliance and attention as a wife,* and resolved to create from its substance a new being, man, who should render to him the most assiduous and devoted service, and to form from it also every variety of animal and vegetable life necessary to man's existence. Tari was filled with jealousy, and attempted to prevent his purpose, but succeeded only so far as to change the intended order of creation.

"The creation was perfectly free from moral and physical evil. Men enjoyed free intercourse with their Creator. They lived without labor upon the spontaneous abundance of the earth; they enjoyed everything in common, and lived in perfect harmony and

* Tradition holds that one of the most flagrant acts of domestic insubordination on the part of Tari consisted in her "refusing to scratch the back of Boora's neck when requested to do so."

peace. They went unclothed. They had power not only to move on the earth, but through the air and the sea. The lower animals were all perfectly innocuous.

"The earthen goddess, highly incensed at the love shown towards man, thus created and endowed, broke into open rebellion against Boora, and resolved to blast the lot of his new creatures by the introduction into the world of every form of moral and physical evil. She instilled into the heart of man every variety of moral evil, 'sowing the seeds of sin in mankind as in a ploughed field,' and, at the same time, introducing every species of physical evil into the material creation, diseases, deadly poisons, and every element of disorder. Boora Pennu, by the application of antidotes, arrested and held in abeyance the elements of physical evil; but he left man perfectly free to receive or to reject moral evil."*

On this one great question, of the contest between Boora and his rebellious consort, the rivalry between the two sects turns. The worshippers of Boora, believing that he proved triumphant in the contest, look to him as the Supreme Being. The sect of Tari, on the other hand, maintaining that she remained unconquered, regard her as the object of divine worship, and hold that she is only to be propitiated by the offering of human victims; hence the Meriah sacrifice prevailed among them. The Boora sect alone practise infanticide; but among them this crime is frightfully prevalent, founded, as is supposed, originally on this idea, that the Sun God, or God of Light (Boora Pennu), contemplating the de-

* Macpherson's Religion of the Khonds, pp. 9, 10.

plorable effects produced to the human race by the female sex, charged that "only so many should be preserved as they could restrain from producing evil to society."* "Again, the Khonds believe that souls almost invariably return to animate human forms in the families in which they have been first born and received. But the reception of the soul of an infant into a family is completed only on the performance of the ceremony of naming upon the seventh day after its birth. The death of a female infant, therefore, before that ceremonial of reception, is believed to exclude its soul from the circle of family spirits, diminishing by one the chance of future female births in the family. And, as the first aspiration of every Khond is to have male children, this belief is a powerful incentive to infanticide."†

But it would appear as if this religious feeling, thus traditionally supposed to have originated the crime, had passed away, and given place to more ordinary work-a-day motives, as if, in reality, the claims of their purses had superseded those of their creed.

The position of women among them, despite this legendary stigma, is very remarkable; their influence

* The reader's memory will naturally suggest to him the analogy between this tradition among a barbarous race and that striking passage in England's greatest epic poem, Paradise Lost, where Adam is represented as so bitterly lamenting the formation of woman as the source of all evil:

"O! why did God,
Creator wise, that peopled highest Heaven
With spirits masculine, create at last
This novelty on earth, this fair defect
Of nature, and not fill the world at once
With men, as angels, without feminine;
Or find some other way to generate
Mankind? This mischief had not then befallen,
And more that shall befal, innumerable
Disturbances on earth through female snares,
And strait conjunction with this sex.

Paradise Lost, b. x. l. 888 to 898.

† Selections, &c., from Records of Government of India, No. 5, p. 67.

and privileges are very great in public as well as in private affairs. Their presence is considered indispensable, and their opinion is of great weight in battle and in council. But in married life their privileges and immunities are preposterous. The paucity of women renders them the more valuable, and therefore they are not to be obtained in marriage without the payment of a very large sum, which is chiefly subscribed by the near relations and the tribe of the bridegroom. The obligations of married life are, on the other hand, most lax; a woman is free to quit her husband at all times, excepting only when pregnant or nursing; and she may transfer her affections as often as the whim takes her. Few women remain constant; it is no merit to do so; many change four or five times in the course of their lives; some more frequently. The only redress or compensation the deserted husband can claim is the repayment of whatever sum was contributed by himself and his tribe on his marriage; the family and tribe of the wife are bound to make this restitution. This violation of marriage contracts is productive of endless difficulty and vexation, and gives rise to innumerable sanguinary quarrels and hereditary feuds. Thus, the Khonds say, "To any man but a rich and powerful chief, who desires to form connexions and is able to make large and sudden restitutions, and to his tribe, a married daughter is a curse. By the death of our female infants before they see the light the lives of men without number are saved, and we live in comparative peace."*

* Macpherson's Account of the Religion of the Khonds, p. 58.

Such are the secret springs of infanticide among these Khonds; the laxity of married life, and the frequent violation of marriage contracts, which their social system recognises, and the vague sanctions of their religious belief.

The arguments used by Captain Macpherson for the suppression of the crime among them are thus briefly described by himself:

"I held, first, that the alleged injunction of the deity, by which the usage is justified, is plainly but a conditional permission, authorising it, at the utmost, only in so far and for so long as the men of any tribe shall find themselves unequal to maintain the peace of society undisturbed through their women; unequal, that is, to the first duties of manhood. The admission of the necessity of the practice by these tribes, necessarily placing them in a position of inferiority to all mankind, who are not compelled, by their incapacity to do justice in questions of property, arising out of the marriages of their daughters, to destroy them in infancy.

"I simply asserted that inquiry will prove the second alleged cause of the usage, viz., the opinion that male births are increased by the destruction of female infants, to be unfounded.

"With respect to the justification, which is laid on the ground that the destruction of infants is a less evil than that which must arise from the contests attendant on the capricious dissolution of their marriages, I held it to be obvious that the practice of infanticide, and the cause of those contests, react upon each other alternately, as cause and effect. Infanticide produces a scarcity of women, which raises marriage payments so high that tribes are easily induced to contest their adjustment, when dissolutions of the tie occur; while these dissolutions are plainly promoted by that scarcity, which prevents every man from having a wife. On the cessation of infanticide women would become abundant, and the marriage payment would become small. Every man would have a wife in these districts, as elsewhere; women would have less power to change, and when they did there would be no difficulty in making the requisite adjustment of property.

"But, lastly, the Government is now about to remove entirely this ground for the practice, by preventing contests about property involved in marriage contracts, by adjudicating all questions respecting it in these districts; thus the evil which infanticide is held to avert will finally cease, and with it all pretence of justification founded on the permissive sanction of the Deity."*

The result of these measures introduced by him, under the sanction of Government, especially the regulation and adjudication of marriage contracts, appeared to be productive of much good; daughters began to appear where they were previously unknown, and in three districts in which the crime had been most prevalent, Captain Macpherson reported, in 1844, that 170 girls had been spared within two years.†

So much in explanation of the principles on which Captain Macpherson acted, and the success which attended them; of his reward, of the recognition of his

* Selections, &c., from Records of Government of India, No. 5, p. 67.

† Ibid. p. 69.

noble services—temporary removal from his post, the victim of petty jealousy between civil and military authorities—nothing need be said.* May others, who, with like single-minded zeal, bear the brunt of such war with evil passions and idolatrous prejudices, have that solace which cheered him "in evil report and in good report,"

"Mens conscia recti;"

and, like his, their reward, though late, will be assuredly reaped in the end.

* See Kaye's Administration of the East India Company, pp. 517 and 518.

APPENDIX.

(Page 3.)

THE following extracts from the sacred books of the Hindoos, the Vedas, and Puranas, will at once show how little sanction they give to the crime of infanticide:

"He who takes pleasure in sin and commits infanticide falls into the great hell called Samisra."

"The man who destroys female infants, Brahmans, and cows, has transgressed all law, and is condemned to dark hells, as long as the fourteen Indras exist."

"He who murders an infant or a Brahman is condemned to those hells which are due punishments to such crimes."

"He who is the destroyer of women (infants), cows, or Brahmans, cannot attain bliss either in this world or the next."

"He who, standing in water, repeats regularly the Gáyatri, may be freed from all other sins, but not from infanticide."

"By repeating ten crores of Gáyatris a man may be

freed from the guilt of killing a Brahman, or of drinking liquor, but never from that of infanticide."

"Killing even a fœtus is as criminal as killing a Brahman; and for killing a female, or woman, the punishment is to suffer in the narak, or hell, called Kat Sutal, for as many years as there are hairs on that female's body; and afterwards that person shall be born again, and successively become a leper, and be afflicted with the Jakhima."

And from another of the Shastras a sloke is often quoted to this effect:

"To kill one Brahman is equal to one hundred cows;

"To kill one woman is equal to one hundred Brahmans;

"To kill one child is equal to one hundred women;

"To kill one hundred children is an offence too grievous for comparison."

(Page 141.)

Copies of three Letters from the Government of India to the Chief Commissioner of the Punjab:

No. 1.—(3894.)

From J. P. Grant, Esq., Officiating Secretary to the Government of India, to J. Lawrence, Esq., Chief Commissioner of the Punjab.

Fort William, Sept. 7, 1853.

Sir,—I have had the honor to receive and lay before the Governor-General in Council your Secretary's despatch of the 8th July, No. 458, forwarding copies of a letter and minute from the Judicial Commissioner, and of a report by Major Edwardes on Female Infanticide in the Punjab.

The Governor-General in Council has read these papers with deep interest and much gratification. He can conceive no purer or higher source of pride for the public officers of a state than such a record as this of the wide and rapid success of their exertions on behalf of the honor of our rule in the rescue of suffering humanity.

The Governor-General in Council desires me to express in the strongest language of cordiality and sincerity the high and grateful approbation with which the Government of India regards exertions on the part of its officers, which are so eminently calculated to reflect honor on the British name, and to add largely to the material happiness of the people whom Providence has lately confided to our care.

I am directed to say, that you and the officers under you may rely with implicit confidence upon the desire of the Governor-General in Council to manifest his appreciation of the wise and benevolent object you have proposed to yourself, and of his readiness to afford you at all times every encouragement and aid which can be supplied by the full measure of his power.

The steps proposed by you, at the suggestion of the Judicial Commissioner, are approved of by his Lordship in Council. Concurring with you in the opinion that anything like open supervision, or secret espionage, on the part of the police should be avoided, as likely to lead to extortion and oppression, the Governor-General in Council is nevertheless of opinion that the sentiments of the Government, in condemnation of this horrible crime, should not be left to make their own way upon the convictions of the people, but should be openly proclaimed and enforced, by denunciation of certain punishment upon those who are convicted of offending.

There are two causes alleged for female infanticide: the one is a religious one, founded upon peculiar tenets, or considerations of caste; the other is a pecuniary one, arising out of the habitual expenditure of large sums upon marriage ceremonies.

The Government can bring its authority to bear upon both causes, by proclaiming that the destruction of female children is murder, whatever may be the moving cause of the crime; and that it shall, in case of conviction, be implacably visited with the punishment justly due to every murderer.

The Governor-General in Council conceives that the suggestion that every Bedee family which receives a pension from the Government should hold it on the condition of pledging itself to the abandonment of this family reproach, is well worthy of consideration at the point to which the question has now attained. Under any circumstances, every such pension should be forfeited where a conviction of infanticide has been pronounced on any family or individual of the Bedees. But his Lordship in Council would go further than this.

The Governor-General in Council will be prepared to sanction any rewards, or honors, or even titles, which you may recommend the Government to bestow upon a few of those who may have been most forward in abandoning the inhuman practices which their fathers pursued.

The second of the two causes of infanticide can only be effectually removed by a voluntary determination of the people themselves to limit, by common consent, the expenses of marriage ceremonies to such amounts as shall do away with all inducement to, or pretext for, the secret destruction of their female children. To this end the proposed great meeting at Umritsur, during the ensuing Dewallee, will no doubt materially conduce. The Governor-General in Council will look with the keenest interest for the reports (which you and your co-adjutors are requested to forward) of the results of this important gathering.

If the Government of India can in any way contribute to the probabilities of success, it will be most ready to do so.

I have, &c.,

J. P. Grant, Officiating Secretary to the Government of India.

No. 2.

From J. P. Grant, Esq., Officiating Secretary to the Government of India, to J. Lawrence, Esq., Chief Commissioner of the Punjab.

Fort William, Feb. 1, 1854.

Sir,—In reply to your Secretary's despatch of the 31st December last, No. 1029, I have the honor to inform you that the Governor-General in Council has read with the deepest interest the report received therewith of the proceedings of the general meeting which was lately held at Umritsur for the purpose of promoting the suppression of the crime of infanticide within the bounds of the Punjab.

The Governor-General in Council has already taken occasion to express the sentiments of high approbation with which the Government of India had seen the exertions of its officers for this noble end. It is most truly gratifying to his Lordship in Council to be able now, after so short an interval, to congratulate them upon the eminent success with which their exertions have already been crowned.

The Governor-General in Council does not think that he overrates the importance of these incidents when he describes the result of the meeting at Umritsur as the commencement of a new social era among the people of the countries beyond the Jumna.

The benevolence, the perseverance, the judgment, and tact by which this harmonious result has been educed from out of such various and discordant materials, are honorable in the highest degree to the gentlemen whose names are enrolled in the record before his Lordship in Council.

To see hereafter the ripening fruit of their present labors will be a higher reward to them than any honor that the Government or the Court of Directors can bestow. Nevertheless, his Lordship in Council desires to renew to them, one and all, an assurance of the interest and deep satisfaction with which the Supreme Government has marked their efforts for good, and of the earnestness with which it will endeavour duly to represent their merits to the Honorable Court.

The report now submitted by you, with selections from

its appendices, will be published immediately, as a number of the selections from the records of the Government of India.

I have, &c.,

J. P. Grant, Officiating Secretary to the Government of India.

No. 3.

From G. F. Edmonstone, Esq., Secretary to the Government of India, to J. Lawrence, Esq., Chief Commissioner of the Punjab.

Fort William, May 25, 1854.

Sir,—I have the honor to acknowledge the receipt of your Secretary's despatch, dated 24th ultimo, No. 335, forwarding a copy of a letter from the Judicial Commissioner, enclosing reports of several meetings held for the suppression of female infanticide in the Mooltan and Jhelum Divisions, and of local meetings of Seealkote and Goojranwalla.

In reply, I am directed to acquaint you that the Governor-General in Council has read with the deepest interest and gratification the reports transmitted by you of the additional meetings which have been held in the Punjab, for devising measures tending to the suppression of the crime of infanticide.

His Lordship in Council has on previous occasions expressed so fully the sense entertained by the Government of the social importance of this object, and of the value of the exertions which the officers of the Government have honorably made for its accomplishment, that his Lordship in Council has only now to repeat the expression of those sentiments in connexion with the proceedings of the Commissioners of Lahore, Jhelum, Mooltan, and Leia.

The success already achieved within the space of a few months has far exceeded the most sanguine anticipations of the Government, and his Lordship in Council ventures to utter a feeling of humble confidence that a blessing will rest on this good work, whereby it shall be made to spread and prosper.

His Lordship in Council requests that you will convey the sincere and cordial thanks of the Government to Mr. Montgomery, the Judicial Commissioner, as well as to the Commissioners, Mr. Raikes, Mr. Thornton, Mr. Edgeworth, and Major Ross; to the Deputy-Commissioners, Mr. Inglis, Mr. Carnac, Captain Brown, and Major Clarke; and to all who have been mentioned with commendation in these reports.

Especially the Governor-General in Council would desire to congratulate Mr. Raikes on the special success of the meeting held near the Seealkote, which gave gratifying proof that the example set by the British Government had been applauded and followed by the foreign state upon our borders.

Meean Runbheer Singh fully deserves all the praise which Mr. Raikes has bestowed upon him; a Khureeta to his address from the Governor-General, and one also to the address of Maharajah Gholab Singh, are herewith forwarded, couched in complimentary and appropriate terms.

I have, &c.,

G. F. Edmonstone, Secretary to the Government of India.

APPENDIX. A GROUND PLAN OF THI

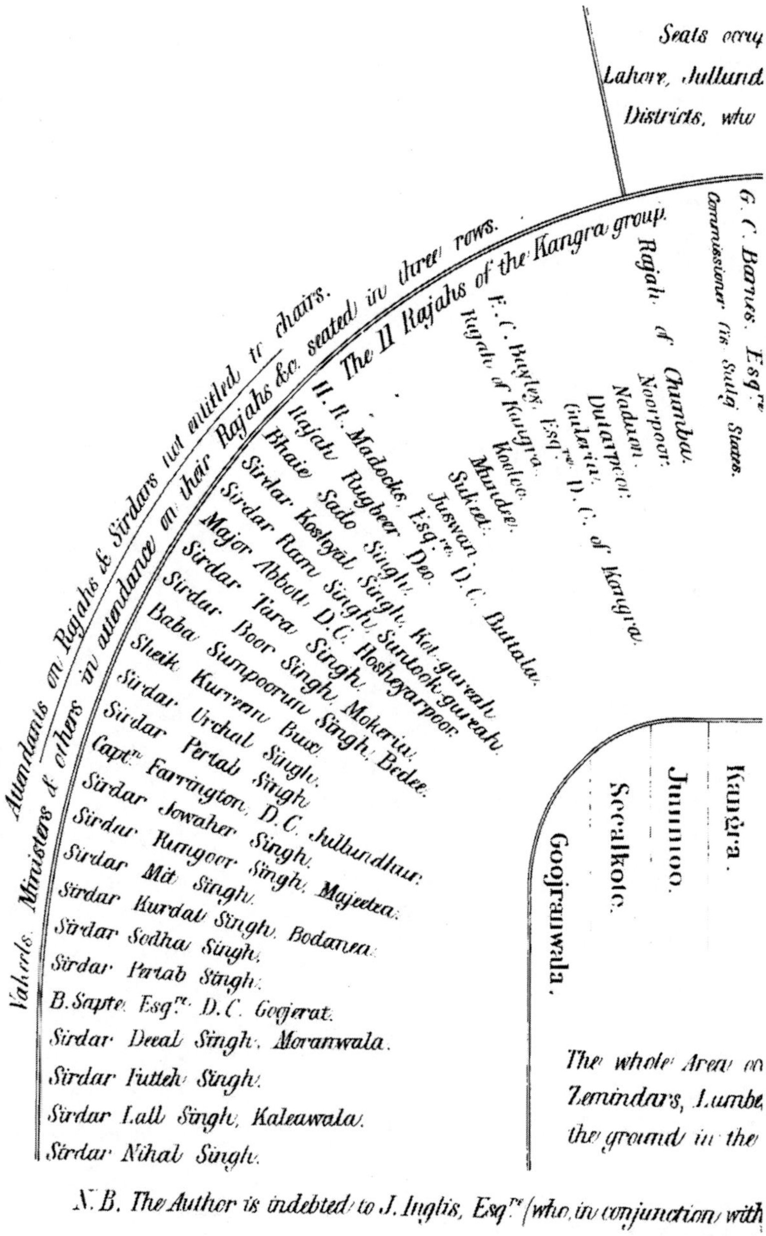

N. B. The Author is indebted to J. Inglis, Esq.re (who, in conjunction with

F. Waller; I

RITSUR MEETING, OCTOBER 31ST. 1853.

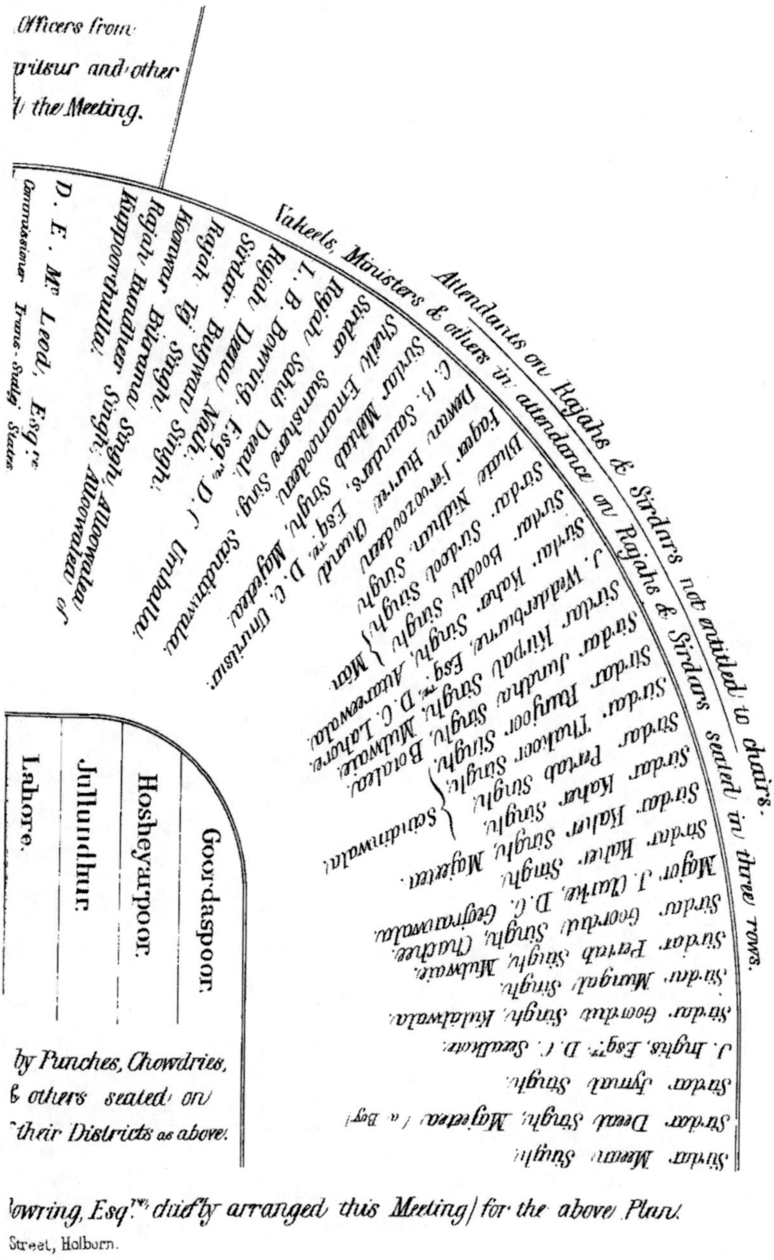

lowring, Esq.re chiefly arranged this Meeting) for the above Plan.

Street, Holborn.

(Page 149.)

Inkar-Nama, or Agreement, on the part of all the Chiefs and People residing in the Punjab and the Trans-Sutlej States, &c., respecting the Prevention of Infanticide and the making of Arrangements in regard to Marriage Expenses. Signed at Umritsur, on the 31st October, 1853.

In the territories of the Punjab the heinous crime of infanticide has not yet been completely suppressed, notwithstanding the existing prohibition issued against it by the authorities. We have, therefore, in accordance with the orders of the Most Noble the Governor-General of India, met together with a view to devise measures for the prevention of the crime; and we hereby make the following engagements, certifying that we shall abide by them:

The crime of infanticide being so hateful to God, and execrable in the eyes of Government and of all pious and good men, we will at once cause the apprehension of any person of our tribe who may perpetrate the crime in our Llakas, or villages, and bring the same to the notice of the authorities; and we will expel from caste any person who may refuse or show reluctance to join in the endeavours to accomplish the above object.

One of the chief causes of infanticide being the expenditure of enormous sums of money on occasions of marriage, in providing for dowries, and for the large number of people who attend at weddings, we shall, with a view to reduce these expenses, adopt in our several castes and tribes all the arrangements connected with marriage charges which are in force in the Mynpooree, Jullundhur, and Hosheyarpore districts, or any other similar arrangements which may be made by Punchayuts, in the presence of the several district officers who preside over us.

Another great evil, besides that of the expenditure above alluded to, is the gathering of Bhâts, Raes, Duts, Bhands, Naees, Meerásees, and beggars, on occasions of marriages, who threaten and abuse the parties concerned in them, and, inflicting injuries on their persons with knives and stones, clamorously demand charity.

If any such party shall in future be found to conduct himself in such an outrageous and harassing manner, he will be apprehended and handed over to the police, and we will never allow him admittance to weddings, or give him anything in charity; and will apply to the district officer for aid in the matter.

Note.—This general agreement was signed at the grand meeting in open Durbar by all the heads of the representatives of the people there assembled.

(Page 150.)

Translation of an Agreement entered into by the Chiefs of the Trans-Sutlej Division, exercising Judicial and Fiscal Powers in their Estates.

A meeting having been assembled at Umritsur, by order of the Most Noble the Governor-General in Council, with a view to devise measures for the complete suppression of infanticide, and to limit the outlay incurred upon marriages, in which meeting I have, by invitation of the British officers, taken part, I hereby engage that the rules agreed to at that meeting shall, in future, be put in force in the estates over which I exercise authority; that I will use my best endeavours entirely to suppress and put an end to the dreadful crime of infanticide; that I will enforce the scale determined upon as the maximum of expenditure to be incurred on occasions of marriage by the different classes over whom I exercise control; and that I will not allow Meerásees, Naees, beggars, or any other class of persons, to exercise importunity at weddings, or in any way to harass those who may be engaged in them.

That if it shall at any time appear that any person has attempted to make the observance of the rules now laid down a subject of reproach or contumely, I will have him brought to punishment; and that I will exert myself generally in all respects, and with hearty good-will, to promote the highly laudable object which the British Government have in view.

Documents to the above effect were separately drawn out in Persian, and signed by the following chiefs:—The Rajah of Alhoowallea, the Rajah of Chumba, and Meean Bhag Singh; and also by the Rajah of Gulehr, with such modifications as were rendered necessary by the fact of his not possessing criminal powers within his estates.

(Page 157.)

The author thankfully avails himself of permission to insert here a letter* addressed in May, 1853, by the Alhoowallea Rajah to D. F. M'Leod, Esq., at that time Commissioner of the Jullundur Division. It is a welcome proof of the civilising influence of English education on the mind of the young Sikh noble—an influence which has almost brought him within the pale of the Christian Church.

Kuppoothulla, May 6, 1853.

"MY DEAR MR. M'LEOD,—The perusal of your letter of the 14th ultimo, and the documents which accompanied it, afforded me the liveliest gratification. I shall make it my duty to give them every circulation, and do my utmost to discountenance the custom and usage hitherto in force in my district, in the prevention by Meerásees and other beggars of acts of insolence or obstructions of any kind on the occasion of marriages; and I hope we may be able to put down the vile custom, which has been the ruin of many, and the vehicle of acts which the poverty of my poor countrymen could not prevent in their families.

"I am aware the above custom has been the means of evils of the grossest description, in the destruction by parents of their own female offspring. It will require a strong arm indeed, and vigilance of no ordinary kind, to

* "This letter," says a friend to whom this young Rajah is well known, "is a genuine autograph, written throughout, as well as signed, by himself." "These two brothers (he goes on to say) refuse to travel on Sundays, or to perform devotions at the shrines of Jawab Nukkti and Kangra; they wished to attend divine service in my house, but were almost forcibly prevented by their followers."

put down this abhorrent practice, and you may rest assured that nothing will be wanting on my part to watch every family that has heretofore been in the habit of committing such unnatural crimes, and to make regular reports of it, should it still be persisted in, and punishing the delinquents most severely. In this country the punishment of one glaring offender of such description will have, in my opinion, the effect of deterring others, and convincing them that the British Government, and other Governments subordinate to it, will visit with condign punishment the perpetrators of such crimes.

"Believe me, my dear Mr. M'Leod,

"Your most sincere friend,

"RUNDHEER SINGH ALUWALLIA.

(Page 191.)

November 24, 1854.

From C. Raikes, Esq., Commissioner Lahore Division, to —— ——, of Seealkote, greeting.

I have learned from an English letter from the Deputy Commissioner of Seealkote, that, agreeably to the admonition of the English Government, and in accordance with your own promise made at Umritsur and Budheeal, you have celebrated the marriage of a daughter at a cost considerably less than that incurred on former occasions; this curtailment of expenditure is a source of great satisfaction to all those in authority, and redounds to your credit.

This is, therefore, given you as a testimonial of approbation that you may keep by you, and that it may incite you to continue your proper economy in the expenditure usual on all occasions of marriages, agreeably to your own promise and the admonitions of the English Government; a course which will lead to your own advantage, and ensure you the approbation of Government.

C. Raikes, Commissioner.

(Page 204.)

Government Notifications.

Legislative Council, 26th July, 1856.

The following Act, passed by the Legislative Council, received the assent of the Right Honorable the Governor-General on the 25th July, 1856, and is hereby promulgated for general information:

Act No. XV. of 1856.

An Act to remove all Legal Obstacles to the Marriage of Hindoo Widows.

Whereas, it is known that, by the law as administered in the Civil Courts established in the territories in the possession and under the Government of the East India Company, Hindoo widows, with certain exceptions, are held to be, by reason of their having been once married, incapable of contracting a second valid marriage, and the offspring of such widows by any second marriage are held to be illegitimate and incapable of inheriting property; and whereas many Hindoos believe that this imputed legal incapacity, although it is in accordance with established custom, is not in accordance with a true interpretation of the precepts of their religion, and desire that the civil law administered by the Courts of Justice shall no longer prevent those Hindoos who may be so minded from adopting a different custom, in accordance with the dictates of their own consciences: and whereas it is just to relieve all such Hindoos from this legal incapacity of which they complain; and the removal of all legal obstacles to the marriage of Hindoo widows will tend to the promotion of good morals and to the public welfare: it is enacted as follows:

I. No marriage contracted between Hindoos shall be invalid, and the issue of no such marriage shall be illegitimate, by reason of the woman having been previously married or betrothed to another person who was dead at the time of such marriage, any custom and any interpretation of Hindoo law to the contrary notwithstanding.

II. All rights and interests which any widow may have in her deceased husband's property by way of maintenance, or by inheritance to her husband, or to his lineal successors, or by virtue of any will or testamentary disposition conferring upon her, without express permission to re-marry, only a limited interest in such property with no power of alienating the same, shall, upon her re-marriage, cease and determine as if she had then died; and the next heirs of her deceased husband, or other persons entitled to the property on her death, shall thereupon succeed to the same.

III. On the re-marriage of a Hindoo widow, if neither the widow nor any other person has been expressly constituted by the will or testamentary disposition of the deceased husband the guardian of his children, the father or paternal grandfather, or the mother or paternal grandmother, of the deceased husband, or any male relative of the deceased husband, may petition the highest Court having original jurisdiction in civil cases in the place where the deceased husband was domiciled at the time of his death, for the appointment of some proper person to be guardian of the said children, and thereupon it shall be lawful for the said Court, if it shall think fit, to appoint such guardian, who, when appointed, shall be entitled to have the care and custody of the said children, or of any of them, during their minority, in the place of their mother; and in making such appointment the Court shall be guided, so far as may be, by the laws and rules in force touching the guardianship of children who have neither father nor mother. Provided that, when the said children have not property of their own sufficient for their support and proper education whilst minors, no such appointment shall be made otherwise than with the consent of the mother, unless the proposed guardian shall have given security for the support and proper education of the children whilst minors.

IV. Nothing in this Act contained shall be construed to render any widow, who, at the time of the death of any person leaving any property, is a childless widow, capable of inheriting the whole or any share of such property, if, before the passing of this Act, she would have been incapable of inheriting the same by reason of her being a childless widow.

V. Except as in the three preceding sections is provided, a widow shall not, by reason of her re-marriage, forfeit any property, or any right to which she would otherwise be entitled; and every widow who has re-married shall have the same rights of inheritance as she would have had, had such marriage been her first marriage.

VI. Whatever words spoken, ceremonies performed, or engagements made, on the marriage of a Hindoo female who has not been previously married; are sufficient to constitute a valid marriage, shall have the same effect if spoken, performed, or made on the marriage of a Hindoo widow; and no marriage shall be declared invalid on the ground that such words, ceremonies, or engagements are inapplicable to the case of a widow.

VII. If the widow re-marrying is a minor, whose marriage has not been consummated, shall not re-marry without the consent of her father, or if she has no father, of her paternal grandfather, or if she has no such grandfather, of her mother, or failing of all these, of her elder brother, or failing also brothers, of her next male relative. All persons knowingly abetting a marriage made contrary to the provisions of this section shall be liable to imprisonment for any term not exceeding one year, or to fine, or to both. And all marriages made contrary to the provisions of this section may be declared void by a court of law. Provided that, in any question regarding the validity of a marriage made contrary to the provisions of this section, such consent as is aforesaid shall be presumed until the contrary is proved, and that no such marriage shall be declared void after it has been consummated. In the case of a widow who is of full age, or whose marriage has been consummated, her own consent shall be sufficient consent to constitute her re-marriage lawful and valid.

THE END.

C. WHITING, BEAUFORT HOUSE, STRAND.